Ramón de Silva Ferro

Historical Account of the Mischances in Regard to the Construction of a Railway Across the Republic of Honduras

Ramón de Silva Ferro

Historical Account of the Mischances in Regard to the Construction of a Railway Across the Republic of Honduras

ISBN/EAN: 9783744696418

Printed in Europe, USA, Canada, Australia, Japan

Cover: Foto ©ninafisch / pixelio.de

More available books at **www.hansebooks.com**

CONTENTS.

	PAGE
NOTE TO THE ENGLISH EDITION	iii
INTRODUCTION	v
I. INTER-OCEANIC ROUTE ACROSS HONDURAS.—HISTORICAL NOTES	1
II. ARRANGEMENT OF THE FEDERAL DEBT.—OTHER CLAIMS AGAINST HONDURAS	6
III. HONDURAS LOAN OF £1,000,000, LONDON, 1867 ...	15
IV. HONDURAS LOAN OF 207,509 BONDS, PARIS, 1869 ...	24
V. HONDURAS LOAN OF £2,500,000, LONDON, 1870 ...	32
VI. PROJECT FOR CONVERTING THE RAILWAY INTO AN INTER-OCEANIC RAILWAY TO TRANSPORT SHIPS	39
VII. MISSION OF A COMMISSIONER TO HONDURAS TO REPORT TO THE PROVISIONAL GOVERNMENT.—ANOTHER LOAN PROJECTED AT PARIS	44
VIII. MEETING OF HONDURAS BONDHOLDERS, 10 JANUARY, 1873	51
IX. MM. HERRAN AND PELLETIER'S ANSWER TO CAPTAIN PIM'S ACCUSATIONS	75
X. MEETING OF BONDHOLDERS, 24 AUGUST, 1873.—FORMATION OF THE HONDURAS INTER-OCEANIC RAILWAY COMPANY	85
XI. CONCLUSION	97

APPENDIX.

No. I. OFFICIAL DOCUMENTS	109
„ II. CUTTING THE TIMBER AND WORKING THE MINES IN HONDURAS	115
„ III. APPENDIX TO THE REPORT OF THE COMMITTEE	117
„ IV. APPENDIX TO THE MEMORANDUM OF ASSOCIATION OF THE HONDURAS INTER-OCEANIC RAILWAY COMPANY ...	132
„ V. SHIP RAILWAY ACROSS CENTRAL AMERICA	138

NOTE TO THE ENGLISH EDITION.

This Historical Account has been written by order of the Honduras Government, communicated to the Minister Plenipotentiary in London, in a dispatch dated Comayagua, the 20th of August, 1874, and received at the Legation in London at the beginning of the following November.

On the 4th of December last, the Minister Plenipotentiary in London directed the Secretary of the Legation to draw up the said Historical Account in accordance with the records in the Archives of the Legation, in time to have it finished and printed, and sent to the Honduras Government by the mail of the 2nd January last, in conformity with the instructions of the said Government, so that it might arrive at Comayagua at the same time as the special Commissioner of the Government, Dr. C. E. Bernhard, who had the direction of all the financial affairs of the Honduras Government in Europe, from the 27th of December, 1872, to the 15th of December, 1874. Dr. Bernhard left Southampton on the 17th of December last, to give a verbal account to the Supreme Government of the Republic of everything connected with the Railway and its loans.

RAMON DE SILVA FERRO,
Secretary of the Honduras Legation.

March, 1875.

TO THE READER.

So much has been written, said, and declaimed on the subject of the construction of a Railway across the Republic of Honduras; so much has this interesting project been opposed, censured, and assailed; so many have been the embarrassments and sudden changes which the various projects formed for this purpose have experienced and undergone; so considerable the failures which have hitherto annihilated every effort to open that Railway; so unsatisfactory, not to say lamentable, the result of the loans contracted to meet the expenses of that costly work; and so various, extraordinary, and frequently injudicious, the public comments upon everything connected with this unfortunate undertaking—that any publication which tends to explain the real causes that have combined against the execution of the Railway across Honduras, meets a pressing necessity, and may serve as a starting-point for ascertaining whether there are still any means of imparting fresh impulse to the work by applying the lessons of the past and adopting a different course to conduct it in future.

It appears that in Europe and in America there has been a fixed and very special design to shun the simple reality of the facts; always setting aside the real cause of all the disasters, to enlarge upon the results only, and, turning round about in a vicious circle, to lay the blame of all that has happened, with as much injustice as temerity, on intermediate entities, which had no more participation in these unfortunate episodes, than an electric wire has in the instructions or transactions which it communicates from one commercial house to another on a different side of the ocean.

The construction of the Honduras Railway has hitherto broken down, because in truth all the combinations which have been attempted for that construction have broken down; because the loans which have been proposed to the public in the European markets have broken down. And why have the loans broken down? Do not those loans amount to more than £5,000,000 sterling? Does not the Government of Honduras still owe that enormous sum? Might not the Railway have been constructed for half that sum? Where have those millions of pounds sterling been buried; where have they found their resting place?

It is by the answers to these questions that the mystery must be solved; but the naked truth is very sad, it is very bitter; and, the truth once known, the fault of the failure falls with equal force upon all who have interests, rights, claims, complaints, or any participation whatever in these matters. It is a kind of *original sin*, which reaches even the most innocent who have anything to do with this undertaking.

The loans failed because they were based upon future guarantees; because their conditions were burdensome and insupportable; because they had not, generally speaking, genuine subscribers. *The nominal sum which those loans represented was never realised, nor even half of it; and that half could not be applied to the construction of the Line because the greater part of it was swallowed up by interest and redemption paid to the bond-holders.* The Government of Honduras complains that it is still liable for considerable loans, the amounts of which it really never received, nor have they been applied to the construction of the Railway,—and it may be added as gospel truth, that they never left the pockets of the speculators; but the Honduras

Government ought to take into account that its special circumstances were dismal in regard to a favourable result of those loans. To those circumstances, which it would be superfluous to mention, must be added the unusual misfortune attendant upon the influence exercised by important political events in Europe and America at the most critical period of each of those operations.

The bond-holders raise loud cries because they are not paid interest at ten per cent. on the nominal capital, and because those bonds which they took *in good faith* are not redeemed at par. Some of the bond-holders, indeed, but very few, subscribed and purchased bonds at the price of issue, in the hope of getting interest for their money at the rate of 13 or 14 per cent. per annum, and they did so in good faith; but nine-tenths of the bond-holders of the Honduras Loans have bought them at 60, at 50, at 40, at 30, at 20, at 10, and at 8 per cent. of their value, in the hope of gaining 20, 30, 60, or 110 per cent. per annum, and with the chance of redemption at par, by which they would gain 100, 200, and even 1150 per cent.; for those who bought bonds at 8 per cent. would gain no less than 1150 per cent., if the bonds were redeemed; and there are many who have obtained them at that price, and even for less.

Those bond-holders who expect such enormous profit, ought to understand that the advantages of speculations are in proportion to the risks which are run of their failure; and, truly, those who speculate on 'Change, and invest their money in public shares which bear 10 per cent. interest, purchasing them for the fifth or the tenth part of their nominal value, ought to suppose that there is great probability of losing their money, and they cannot complain if that probability becomes a fact.

Here, then, we have the two extremes, altogether anomalous, which are the real cause of the failures in regard to the Honduras Railway; the Government, which expected to obtain loans for the construction of that work, on conditions very difficult to fulfil; and the bond-holders, who, relying on suicidal usury, have made that impossible which was only very difficult, by reducing the value of those bonds to a ruinous price, at which they received them from the trustees of the Government or from their agents.

In short, the Government thought it could accomplish the construction of the Railway by recourse to European loans which it expected to obtain easily, without any sacrifice, without any mischance, without any effort on its part, confiding in the utility of the enterprise and in its future proceeds; and the European lenders have tried to obtain a colossal profit, by getting the bonds of the Honduras Government, representing amounts of which only a small part has been paid; thus ruining the purpose of the Government in soliciting those loans, and paying dear themselves for their boundless ambition.

These two extremes, equally vicious in principle, have been united by a chain of intermediaries and fellow-workers on both sides, who have stood the brunt of those opposing forces, frequently falling into a whirlwind of confusion, of difficulty, and deception, without knowing how to get out of it. Not all, perhaps, have conducted themselves with the uprightness, with the enthusiasm, disinterestedness, and self-denial, which are required to overcome great inconveniences. These qualifications are preeminent in the enlightened Hondurean D. Leon Alvarado, one of the principal promoters of this undertaking; but the evils referred to were inevitable consequences of the very serious circumstances, and they would not have existed if the means by which it was intended to construct such an enormous work had been a little more solid and to the purpose.

So many forces have conspired against the success of the Honduras Railway that even a moiety of them would have sufficed to ruin any undertaking. It is not necessary to take into account the peculiar circumstances of the Republic, and the incessant revolutions to which it has been subject; it is enough to mention the external causes.

Almost all those interested in other inter-oceanic lines across America have conspired against the success of the Railway; the bond-holders themselves, and all the speculators at the Exchanges where the loans were announced, have conspired against it; misfortune, with wars and public calamities in her train, which prejudiced the operations, has conspired against it; former creditors of Honduras for comparatively insignificant sums, in order to avail themselves of the opportunity of getting payment by this means, have conspired against it; unworthy speculators without conscience, who derive profit by calculating upon the fall in matters which have not the proper solidity, have conspired against it; many persons who ought not to have conspired, have conspired, for the pleasure of doing mischief, and not a few from ignorance; and many others have conspired against it for the sole purpose of getting paid for the damage they could do.

The historical account which follows hereafter fully explains the principal events connected with the Honduras Railway and its loans. It is based upon authentic documents and drawn up with impartiality, not with the intention of attacking or defending any persons who have been mixed up in these affairs with more or less chances, with more or less misfortune, but for the purpose of affording a little more enlightenment to the present Government of Honduras, and also for the information of some private persons who are not sufficiently acquainted with these matters, and who lose themselves in a sea of conjectures, because they see nothing below the surface.

London, January 1, 1875.

HISTORICAL ACCOUNT.

I.

INTER-OCEANIC ROUTE ACROSS HONDURAS.— HISTORICAL NOTES.

The magnificent maritime ports which Honduras possesses in the Atlantic and Pacific Oceans, namely, Port Caballos and the Bay of Fonseca, originated the idea of a grand route for communication between the two oceans, as early as the middle of the sixteenth century, scarcely half a century after the discovery of America.

The first serious survey for a road across Honduras from Port Caballos to the Bay of Fonseca, was made in 1555 by Juan Garcia de Hermosilla, by order of the King of Spain.

In the year 1586 the celebrated Italian engineer, Baptista Antonelli, who erected the castle of San Juan de Ulloa, and that of the Morro at Havannah, was commissioned to survey the route across Honduras in conjunction with the Spaniard Juan de Tejada. They surveyed and sounded the ports at both extremities of the projected line, and they made a splendid report in favour of that inter-oceanic way. Many other surveys were made for the same purpose in the 17th century; and if the opening of that road was not executed by the Spaniards, it was because rivalries had already grown up there, resulting from private interests, and because for the time the difficulty prevailed, arising from the fact that the ports of Caballos and Fonseca were too spacious to be put in a state of defence, so that ships which were anchored in them might be secure and safe from the attacks of the pirates who then infested those coasts.

The discovery of the auriferous mines of California and the immense importance which the emigration from Europe and the United States to the Western shores of the Pacific, acquired from that time, again introduced the problem which for a very long time before had occupied the attention of the Spaniards; that is, the choice of the best route across Central America, or the Isthmus of Darien, for the construction of a railway or the cutting of a canal which should fully meet the requirements of commerce and the transit of passengers.

In the years 1850 to 1852 the representative of the United States in Central America, Mr. E. G. Squier, conceived the idea that it might be possible to make a railway across the Republic of Honduras from Port Caballos to the Bay of Fonseca. Adhering to this idea, he succeeded in getting a scientific body organised in the United States to ascertain the practicability of that line. That body left the United States in February, 1853, and returned in December of the same year. The report was very favourable; and, in consequence, Mr. Squier solicited from the Government of Honduras a concession for the construction of the road, in favour of Messrs. Robert J. Walker, Amory Edwards, A. Miltenberger, James S. Thayer, Henry Stanton, Fletcher Westray, and E. G. Squier himself. General D. José Trinidad Cabañas was then President of the Republic, and D. Leon Alvarado and D. Justo F. Rodas were the Commissioners of the said Government.

Having obtained from the Government of Honduras the concession to construct this Railway, on the 28th of July, 1853, Mr. Squier formed a company in New York, which broke up shortly after on account of the opposition which it met with from those who were interested in and partisans of the Panama Line, and on account of the contempt and indifference with which it was received by the speculating public of the United States.

The promoters of this undertaking determined to have recourse to the European markets, in order to seek funds to carry it out. For this purpose they commissioned its originator Mr. Squier, to proceed to London or Paris, and bring it before the public in one of those capitals.

After two years of contest and exertion, overcoming difficulties and opposition, he succeeded in forming a mixed Company, that is, English, French, and North American, with its seat in London, and under the direct sanction of the English Government. Sir William Brown figured in that Company as President, and Robert Wigram Crawford, Esq., as Vice-President, besides many other eminent men of high social position not surpassed by those of any other Company.

Here is the complete list of the gentlemen who formed that Company; and who, by their social position, influence, and wealth, constitute an association so respectable and powerful, that no better could be assembled at any place in the commercial world :—

SIR WILLIAM BROWN, Bart.
R. W. CRAWFORD, Esq., M.P., London.
ABRAHAM DARBY, Esq., Stoke Court, Slough.
JOHN PEMBERTON HEYWOOD, Esq. (Heywood, Kennards, & Co.), Lombard Street.
CHARLES HOLLAND, Esq., President of the Liverpool Chamber of Commerce.
THOMAS SANDEN KIRKPATRICK, Esq., London.
M. T. WEGUELIN, Esq., London.
CHARLES F. MOULTON, Esq., Paris.
JOHN LEWIS RICARDO, Esq., M.P., London.
Major-General TREMENHERE, London.
WILLIAM WHEELWRIGHT, Esq., London.
JOSEPH ROBINSON, Esq., Ebbw Vale Company.

It was Lord Clarendon himself, then Minister for Foreign Affairs of Great Britain, who induced Sir William Brown to undertake the Presidentship of the Company, and gave, on his part, all the facilities in his power in order that the construction might be carried on.

On the 20th of August, 1856, a Treaty of Friendship, Commerce, and Navigation was concluded between Great Britain on the one part, represented by Lord Clarendon, and the Republic of Honduras on the other part, represented by the Minister of Honduras in London. That treaty established the neutrality of the Railway across Honduras, under the protection of Great Britain, with other conditions favourable to the development of commerce and free-trade by the said Line. The United States and France concluded similar treaties soon afterwards.

By another treaty of 28th November, 1859, in consideration of the peculiar geographical position of Honduras, and to secure the neutrality of the adjacent islands with reference to any Railway or inter-oceanic Line across Honduras, her Britannic Majesty's Government agreed to recognise the islands of Roatan, Helena, Barbarota, Guanajo, Utila, and Morat, known as the Bay Islands, and situated in the Gulf of Honduras, as an integral part of the said Republic.

By another article of the same Treaty, the English Government recognised the sovereignty of the Republic of Honduras over the territory inhabited by the Mosquito Indians, comprised within the limits of the frontier of the said Republic, whatever they might be.

In this manner the difficulties were amicably settled which existed between Great Britain, Central America, and the United States.

This restitution of the Bay Islands and the Mosquito Territory to the Republic of Honduras, on the part of England, was the first advantage which Honduras obtained from the project of opening an Inter-oceanic Railway across its territory.

The Company having been formed in London, and at the

personal expense of its directors, who laid out some £80,000 upon it, a complete survey of the Line was made in the years 1857 and 1858, under the direction of General William W. Wright, and the ports and rivers were carefully surveyed by Captain W. N. Jeffers, of the United States Navy. These labours were then verified by Lieutenant-Colonel Edward Stanton, Royal Engineer, who, with a body of engineers under his orders, was sent to Honduras in the service of Her Britannic Majesty's Government.

The survey of the whole line of the Railway was minutely explained in the following collection of documents:—

 I. General Map of the whole line of the proposed Railway from Port Caballos (or Cortez) to the Bay of Fonseca, upon a scale of a mile to an inch.
 II. Detailed Topographical Maps of the field of labour (24 Maps) on a scale of 500 feet to an inch.
 III. Profile or vertical section of the whole line, on a scale of 400 feet to an inch horizontal, and 40 feet vertical.
 IV. Detailed Chart of the part of the Bay of Fonseca where the Railway is to terminate, drawn from triangulations by Lieutenant Jeffers, Hydrographical Engineer.
 V. Detailed Chart of Port Caballos and Alvarado Lagoon.
 VI. Extracts from the Memoir, by J. C. Trautwine, Esq., Chief Engineer.
 VII. Memoir by W. W. Wright, Esq., First Assistant Engineer, containing tables and details of the cuttings, embankments, tunnels, bridges, &c., with the estimates.
 VIII. Memoir by Lieutenant W. N. Jeffers, of the United States Navy, respecting the Bay of Fonseca.
 IX. Memoranda and observations presented by Lieutenant W. N. Jeffers, acting as deputed agent.
 X. Extract from the Memoir by Lieutenant Colonel Edward Stanton to General Sir J. F. Burgoyne, K.C.B., respecting the Bay of Fonseca.
 XI. Memoir by Dr. J. L. Le Conte, respecting the agricultural and mineral resources of the country in the vicinity of the line of railway.
 XII. Memoir by Gustavus Holland, M.D., Surgeon to the expedition.

XIII. Extract from a Memoir addressed to the French Government, respecting the Bay of Fonseca, by Captain M. T. de Lapelin, of the Frigate "La Brillante."

But before the fruits of these preparatory labours could be gathered, the Italian War broke out, and all the operations for carrying on the undertaking were suspended. Then also began the war in the United States, and very soon after the invasion of Mexico by the French; and under these circumstances the directors of the Company in London, who had, moreover, received from one of their engineers an unfavourable report in regard to the practicability of the Line, lost heart, and suspended all action calculated for the furtherance of the undertaking.

In the midst of so many unfavourable circumstances, the concession for the said Railway became void, by virtue of one of the articles contained therein, and the projected Honduras Railway disappeared for the time from the public stage.

II.

ARRANGEMENT OF THE FEDERAL DEBT.—OTHER CLAIMS AGAINST HONDURAS.

AFTER the lapse of some time, D. Leon Alvarado, a worthy son of Honduras, who had signed the original concession in the name of the Government of the Republic, came to Europe as Special Commissioner of that Government, and tried in vain to re-organize the Company on the same basis as before. But his efforts produced not the slightest result; and it was then decided to have direct recourse to the English public, and solicit a loan in the name of the Government of Honduras, for the purpose of applying it to the construction of the Railway; offering as security for the said loan, not only the Line itself which it was intended to construct, but also the uncultivated lands and the magnificent forests of the Republic.

The first difficulty which stood in the way of this project was that, according to the regulations of the London Exchange, no foreign nation which has not fulfilled its previous financial engagements, or has not arranged them satisfactorily with its creditors, can enter into fresh negociations in the monetary market, or quote funds of new loans or undertakings on the said Exchange.

The Government of Honduras was endeavouring to arrange the part which had been assigned to it in the partition of the Federal debt of Central America, amongst the five independent Republics which were formed after the dissolution of the Federation, which Federal debt originated as follows :—

In August 1825, the then Federal States of Central America, namely, Guatemala, Honduras, Salvador, Nicaragua, and Costa Rica, proposed to negotiate a loan in London of £1,428,571 nominal value; but only £163,300 were issued, at six per cent· annual interest.

When the federation was dissolved, the five States which had composed it divided this debt amongst them, according to Mr. Chatfield's arrangement, the share of each of them being as follows :—

Honduras, two-twelfths	£27,200
Guatemala, five-twelfths	67,900
Salvador, two-twelfths	27,200
Nicaragua, two-twelfths	27,200
Costa Rica, one-twelfth	13,500
Which items amount to	£163,000

From February 1827 to April 1844, none of the five States of Central America paid the interest on the part of the debt which had been assigned to it.

In April 1844, Costa Rica made an arrangement of its part with the English creditors, paying them 85 per cent. of the capital; thus the creditors lost the remaining 15 per cent. and seventeen years' interest.

In 1856, that is, twelve years after Costa Rica, Guatemala made an arrangement of its debt, paying the English creditors 61 per cent. of the capital and the interest for twenty-seven years overdue—not in coin, however, but in bonds issued for the purpose, which bore an annual interest of five per cent. instead of the six per cent. on the previous bonds.

Four years after Guatemala, that is in 1860, Salvador was the third State which arranged with its creditors. During the years 1860, 1861, and 1862, it paid them in coin up to 90 per cent. of the capital of the debt, and the creditors lost 10 per cent. of the capital, and the interest for thirty-four years.

Nicaragua has not paid the interest on its part of the Federal debt since 1827, and only lately, in 1873 and 1874, has it taken steps to make an arrangement.

The Federal debt belonging to Honduras, with the interest overdue, amounted in July, 1867, to 231 per cent. of the original capital, that is, to £62,862 for interest, which with the capital made a total of £90,075.

D. Leon Alvarado then saw himself under the imperative necessity of arranging this debt, because without such previous arrangement nothing—absolutely nothing—could be attempted in regard to the projected loans for the construction of the Railway. Besides the Federal debt, there was a claim of the firm of Hart for the sum of £7,300, arising from a sale of guns to the Government; and this firm opposed every negotiation of Honduras in the market, unless an arrangement were also made with it in regard to that debt.

Then the creditors of the Federal debt held a meeting, and the Commissioner of the Government proposed to them as an arrangement, to acknowledge £55,000 for capital and interest, instead of the £90,075 capitalised; on condition of paying the £55,000 by giving new bonds for the said sum, which were to bear an annual interest of 5 per cent. At the same time there was no other remedy but to pay the firm of Hart its claim, or at least to give it security for payment with the same kind of bonds; and besides it was necessary that the operation should provide for the expenses of commission, of drawing the bonds, and some others, to commence the operations which were contemplated for the Railway.

So the arrangement was made by issuing £90,000 nominal in bonds with 5 per cent. interest, which bonds were distributed in the following manner:—

To the former holders of bonds of the Federal debt, new bonds were delivered to the value of . . .	£55,000*
With Messrs. Hart & Co. new bonds were deposited as security for their effective claim of £7,300 to the amount of	15,000
Delivered to the Commissioner, Señor Don Leon Alvarado, for expenses, &c. including £2,000 in bonds to Mr. Haslewood the broker . . .	20,000
Total amount of bonds issued to pay the old Federal debt of Honduras	£90,000

It was intended to redeem these bonds in due course, with funds which would be destined for the purpose, arising from the loans intended for the construction of the Railway, in accordance with the powers and instructions sent by the Government; and as a security for the fulfilment of this arrangement the revenues of the Custom-house of Amapala were pledged, upon which there was already a lien by order of Congress for the pending debt of Messrs. Hart.

It should be borne in mind that there are in England some other claims against the Government of Honduras, which are under the official safeguard of the English Government. One, called the Carmichael claim, dates from 1852, and amounts to 54,830 dollars, as was allowed by the commission which assembled at Guatemala, in 1862, to decide respecting the English claims against Honduras, in accordance with the convention, signed at Comayagua, on the 28th of November, 1859, known by the name of the "Mosquito Convention." The Honduras Government offered to pay that sum to the representatives of Mr. Carmichael in mahogany; but was not able to fulfil that arrangement, and the English Government has in consequence made serious and repeated reclamations which are still pending.

Mr. Carmichael has also another pending claim against the Government of Honduras for 15,000 dollars, according to the convention called "Chatfield-Cruz," signed in 1852, for the payment of which and of other lesser claims included in the same convention, the proceeds of the Custom-houses of Trujillo and Omoa were pledged to Sir C. Wyke in 1856. This claim of Carmichael, and others which are annexed to it, amount without interest to the sum of 26,761 dollars, on account of which sum, according to a memorandum of Lord Granville's, dated 5th June, 1873, the Government of Great Britain has received 3,345 dollars 81¼ cents, proceeding from the Custom-houses of Trujillo and Omoa, and £1800, or 9000 dollars, paid on account by the Minister in London, Señor Gutierrez.

There is also a third claim of the English Government against the Government of Honduras still pending, which arises from the stipulation in the Treaty between Her Britannic Majesty and the said Republic, signed at Comayagua, on the 28th of November, 1859, the ratifications of which were exchanged, at Comayagua, on the 18th April, 1860, by which Treaty the British Government has transferred the Bay Islands and the Mosquito Territory to Honduras. The second paragraph of Article III. of the said Treaty reads textually thus:—

"The Republic of Honduras wishing to educate the Mosquito Indians, and to improve their social condition in the district occupied by them, will grant an annual sum of *five thousand dollars* in silver or gold, during the next ten years, for that purpose, which shall be paid to the chief of the Moscos in that district, that payment being guaranteed by a lien upon all the timber and upon all the other natural products (whatever they may be) of the uncultivated lands in the Bay Islands and in the Mosquito territory.

"These payments shall be made by half-yearly instalments of 2,500 dollars each; the first of these payments shall be made six months after the exchange of the ratifications of the present Treaty."

During all the time that has elapsed since the Bay Islands were transferred to Honduras, only one instalment of £500 has been paid by the Minister of Honduras in London, D. Carlos Gutierrez: this was to the British Minister, Lord Russell, on the 26th of August, 1861; but both this instalment, and the £1,800 paid on account of the Carmichael claim, came from the funds of the loans, which will be spoken of further on, contracted for the construction of the Honduras Railway.

In order to conclude the history of the so-called "Federal debt," it is necessary to anticipate some facts, without attending to their chronological order.

Since the arrangement of the debt was made, the following sums have been regularly paid to redeem the bonds of the said debt, and this from funds taken from subsequent loans for the construction of the Railway.

Redemption of the Federal Debt, according to the Arrangement of 1867.

October, 1868, redeemed at par	£1,500
April, 1869 ,, ,,	800
October, 1869 ,, ,,	850
April, 1870 ,, ,,	850
October, 1870 ,, ,,	900
April, 1871 ,, ,,	1,000
October, 1871 ,, ,,	1,400
April, 1872 ,, ,,	1,450
October, 1872 ,, ,,	2,400
Redeemed at par	£11,150

From this it appears that £11,150 of the Federal debt (which was, as has been said, £90,000 nominal) having been redeemed, there remains the sum of £78,850 to be redeemed.

Moreover, five entire years of interest of the said debt, at the annual rate of 5 per cent., have been paid, that is, the years 1868, 1869, 1870, 1871, and 1872, which payment has required £21,550 cash; so that, to meet the interest and the reduction of the Federal debt during five years, the following sums have been paid in London on account of the Republic of Honduras:—

For five years' interest	£21,550
For redemption, 5 years	11,150
Total paid	£32,700

It is needless to say that these £32,700 were taken from the produce of the loans for the construction of the Railway; and the regular payment of this debt, so far as was possible, could on no account be neglected, because of the absolute necessity of maintaining the credit of the Republic in London, in order not to find in those creditors powerful enemies who

ERRATUM.

Page 12, line 3, *for* " at par," *read* " at market price."

might oppose the operations necessary for the completion of the Railway, according to the orders of the Honduras Government.

So soon as the payment of the interest and the redemption of this debt ceased, which was in April, 1873, Messrs. Hart, who had the value of £15,000 in bonds in their possession, and who had been receiving the interest upon those bonds, peremptorily insisted that their claim should be paid to them in cash. It was necessary to do this. Under a fresh agreement they were paid £6,000 in cash to cancel their claim, and they then returned the £15,000 in bonds, which they held in deposit as a guarantee, and which now belong to the Government of Honduras, and are in the possession of Mr. Edward Haslewood, as may be seen by the following account of the present state of the said Federal debt.

State of the Federal Debt of Honduras on the 1st of January, 1874.

Total amount of the bonds issued for the arrangement of the Federal debt in 1867		£90,000
Deduct the Bonds redeemed at par, from 1868 to 1872, both inclusive .		11,150
Remains unredeemed . .		£78,850
In possession of Mr. Edward Haslewood, returned by Hart	£15,000	
Balance of those delivered to D. Leon Alvarado, for payment of Commission, &c. &c. . . .	2,900	
Belonging to the Government . .		17,900
Remaining in Circulation . . .		£60,950

The sum of £17,900 in bonds of the Federal debt, which belong to the Government, may be cancelled whenever it chooses; and in that case the bonds still remaining for redemption will be reduced to £60,950, the amount of those in circulation. But it must be borne in mind that there are two years' interest already due upon those bonds, which amount approximately to some £8,000. It may also happen, although it is not probable, that the Government may put the £17,900 in bonds above-mentioned into circulation again, in which case the Federal debt to be redeemed would mount up to £78,850.

Before concluding this Chapter, it will be well to give a brief statement of the sums already mentioned as having been paid in London on account of the debts in arrear of the Republic of Honduras, in order to maintain its credit in the English market, and all those taken from the funds of the loans intended for the construction of the Railway :—

Interest and Redemption of the Federal Debt, payments made from 1868 to 1872	£32,700
Debt paid to Hart	6,000
Paid to Lord Russell for one Instalment for the Mosquito Indians	500
Paid to Lord Granville on account of the Claim of Carmichael and others	1,800
	£41,000

If these £41,000 had been applied to the construction of the Railway, they would have been sufficient for eleven miles of the said Line.

III.

HONDURAS LOAN OF ONE MILLION STERLING.—
LONDON, 1867.

WHEN the difficulty of the Federal debt had been arranged in 1867, attention began to be paid to the basis for the first loan to be applied to the construction of the Railway, the Government of Honduras being represented therein by its own Commissioner, D. Leon Alvarado, and by the two accredited ministers of the Republic at Paris and in London, Monsieur Herran and Señor Gutierrez.

It will be easily understood that the Republic of Honduras had not that state of material development, density of population, favourable condition of finances, organised resources, or industry and commerce, to be in the most appropriate position for the issue of a loan of *a million sterling*, with probabilities of success in the English market; that is, a loan thirty-six times greater than that part of the Federal debt belonging to Honduras, which had just been arranged, and the interest on which the Republic had neither been able to pay, nor to give anything on account of it for forty years, although the amount of that interest was then only £1,632 a year.

Besides, what guarantees, what pledges, what securities satisfactory to the public could they offer who were commissioned to launch that loan on the market in the name of the Government of Honduras?

The revenues of the Custom-houses of Omoa, Trujillo, and Amapala, which are very moderate and absolutely necessary to the Government itself, to provide for the necessities of its administration, were already pledged; besides, they would not suffice to guarantee a loan of a twentieth part of that sum.

Nevertheless, the construction of the Inter-oceanic Railway across Honduras is of such vital importance to the commerce of the whole world and to the future lot of that Republic, and the mere idea of initiating that important work so alluring, that it appeared to the Government, as well as to all the enthusiasts for that Line, that, though not easy, it was at least possible to overcome all the difficulties by perseverance, assiduity, and energy; so, in spite of those difficulties, and in the hope of overcoming them, it was determined to launch a first loan of a million sterling on the London market.

To introduce loans of this kind to the monetary markets of Europe, whatever may be the purpose of such loans, it is the established custom to arrange the conditions of them with some banking-house of great reputation, which introduces and conducts the operation, and undertakes, if so agreed, all the preliminary expenses and gives credit to the operation, taking more or less interest therein for a commission of so much per cent. which is offered to it and forms part of the terms of the arrangements, and frequently receiving also a certain number of bonds at a lower price than that stipulated for offering them to the public.

Generally the public does not care to investigate the reserved conditions upon which the banking-house introduces the loan, nor yet to dive into the validity of the guarantees or pledges which the house has accepted for launching the loan. The public very specially regards the name and position of the house which conducts the operation, and takes it for granted that when a respectable house lends its name for the management of such an operation, and for the consequent combinations in the market, it must have well and minutely studied the securities and risks of the operation.

The antecedents which have been referred to in regard to the economical position and the resources of Honduras, kept back those bankers who usually manage such operations. Nevertheless, after many favourable reports, arguments, and efforts, the influential banking-house of Messrs. Bischoffsheim, Goldschmidt, & Co., taking into consideration the great utility of the projected Railway, and the purpose of the loan, consented to undertake the management of the operation, after stipulating the conditions with the two Ministers of Honduras, who had received instructions and powers to that effect.

The Prospectuses of the first Honduras loan of £1,000,000 appeared in July, 1867. It was divided into bonds of £100, £500, and £1,000, with 10 per cent. annual interest payable half-yearly; 3 per cent. sinking fund, so as to be redeemed in seventeen years; and the price of issue was 80 per cent.—that is, that for each £100 bond which the public subscribed for, £80 were to be paid, which, after certain deductions for interest on the various instalments, were reduced in reality to £73. 11s. 10½d. for every nominal £100. The subscription was to be paid in six instalments, the first on subscribing and the last on the 1st April, 1869. This arrangement was made to give the public every kind of security for the subscription, and also to provide that no interest should become due except upon the money actually employed.

To explain the matter more fully, here is the Prospectus of the said loan:—

"HONDURAS GOVERNMENT RAILWAY LOAN,

"£1,000,000.

"*In Bonds to Bearer, of £100, £500, and £1,000 each, bearing 10 per cent. Annual Interest, payable half-yearly in sterling.*

"*Issued at 80 per cent., and to be redeemed at par, in sterling, within 17 years, by Yearly Drawings, by means of an Accumulative Sinking Fund of 3 per cent. per annum.*

"The first Drawing will take place on December 31st, 1869.

"The payments by Subscribers will be as follows:—

				£. s. d.	£. s. d.
5 per cent.	on application				5 0 0
10 ,,	on allotment				10 0 0
10 ,,	on January 1st, 1868, less interest			0 9 4½	9 10 7½
15 ,,	on July 1st, 1868, less interest			1 11 3	13 8 9
20 ,,	on January 1st, 1869, less interest			2 10 0	17 10 0
20 ,,	on April 1st, 1869, less interest			1 17 6	18 2 6
80 per cent.					£73 11 10½

"Interest will be payable on the 1st July and the 1st January in each year, at the London and County Bank, and, for the first instalment of £15, will date from 1st October, 1867.

"In default of payment of any of the respective instalments, all previous payments will be liable to forfeiture.

"The instalments may be anticipated at any time at Bank of England rate.

"The Government of Honduras having agreed to appropriate to the Subscribers a moiety of the net profits of the Railway during 15 years after the complete repayment of the present Loan, Subscribers will receive as bonus, within one month after allotment, with each £100 Bond, one 10,000th deferred fully paid-up Railway Share to Bearer, entitling the holder thereof to receive his proportion of such net profits.

"PROSPECTUS.

"The President of the Republic of Honduras, being duly authorized, has given full powers to Mons. Victor Herran, Minister at Paris, and Señor Don Carlos Gutierrez, Honduras Minister in London, to contract on account of the Government a Loan, to be applied towards the construction of an Inter-oceanic Railway from Puerto Caballos, on the Atlantic, to the Bay of Fonseca, on the Pacific.

"To show the importance attached by the British Government to the Honduras Inter-oceanic Railway, it may be stated that the line has been surveyed on the part of Her Majesty's Government, by Lieutenant-Colonel Stanton, R.E., and a detachment of Royal Engineers sent out for the purpose. Colonel Stanton reports, 'that the harbours at both termini are unexceptionable,' and that the road can be constructed 'without any sharper curves or heavier gradients than are to be found on existing lines over which locomotives work without difficulty.'

"The new Treaty between Honduras and Great Britain declares that,—

> 'In order to secure the construction and permanence of 'the route or road herein contemplated, and to secure for 'the benefit of mankind the uninterrupted advantages of 'such communication from sea to sea, Her Britannic 'Majesty recognizes the rights of sovereignty and property 'of Honduras in and over the line of the said road, and for 'the same reason guarantees, positively and efficaciously, 'the entire neutrality of the same. And when the pro-'posed road shall have been completed, Her Britannic 'Majesty equally engages, in conjunction with the Republic 'of Honduras, to protect the same from interruption, 'seizure, or unjust confiscation, from whatsoever quarter 'the attempt may proceed.'

"Treaties signed by the Honduras Government with France and the United States contain the same provisions, and the French Government, considering the public utility of the Honduras Railway, has promised the official quotation of the Honduras Loan on the Paris Bourse.

"The following official report by Rear-Admiral Davis, made to the Secretary of the Navy of the United States Government, in compliance with a resolution of the American Congress on the 19th of March, 1866, demonstrates likewise the importance which the United States Government attaches to the construction of the Honduras Line :—

> 'The reader who follows the course of the surveyors, 'naturalists, and geologists from the capacious, safe, and 'excellent harbour of Puerto Caballos, through regions 'remarkable for their salubrity, fertility, great variety of 'climate and productions, and valuable mineral resources, 'to the waters of the splendid harbour of La Union (Bay of 'Fonseca), cannot but regret that capitalists have not found 'it to their interest to carry out one of the most promising 'and one of the least embarrassing enterprises of the day.'

"The Line of Railway has been carefully selected and surveyed by Mr. Trautwine (late Engineer-in-Chief of the Panama Railway), and an efficient staff; and a contract has been entered into for the construction of the whole Line, with Stations and Rolling Stock, for a stipulated sum of about £8000 a mile, including every outlay, and the works are to be proceeded with in sections.

"From time to time, as the instalments of the present loan are received, the proportion to be applied to the construction of the first section of the Railway will be handed to and held by trustees, in trust to pay the contractor the instalments on his contract, as certified by the Government Engineer. The balance of the loan will be applied in clearing the forests, and in payment of engineering and other incidental expenses.

"The Interest and Sinking Fund of the Loan are specially guaranteed by a first charge upon the intended Railway itself and its revenue, and also by a first mortgage upon the whole of the domains and mahogany forests of the State of Honduras, which, according to official report, are of immense value.

"It is arranged that the whole of the produce of the above mortgaged State Domains and Forests shall be consigned direct to London by the Honduras Government, to Messrs. Bischoffsheim and Goldschmidt, who will pay over the proceeds of the sales towards the Annual Interest and Sinking Fund, and the construction of the remaining sections of the Railway.

"It has been further arranged in the contract, that, as soon as any portion of the Railway is completed, the Contractor shall bring down to the Terminus, free of charge, by the return empty waggons, any produce of the Government Forests and Domains that may be ready for shipment to England.

"Beginning at the harbour of Puerto Caballos, on the Atlantic, the Railway will proceed over the table-land of Honduras, in a line of 230 miles, to the Bay of Fonseca, on the Pacific.

"The ports at either end are spacious, safe, and easily accessible for the largest ships.

"The steaming distances from Liverpool to San Francisco, touching at Jamaica, are:—by way of Panama, 7,980 miles; Nicaragua, 7720 miles; Tehuantepec, 7740 miles; Honduras, 7320 miles.

"The distance between New York and San Francisco, by Panama, is 5224 miles; by Nicaragua, 4700 miles; by Tehuantepec, 4200 miles; by Honduras, 4121 miles—a saving by way of Honduras, as compared with Panama, the only Line on which a Railway is already constructed, of 1103 miles.

"The difference in actual distance, coupled with the superiority of ports, the facilities of embarkation and disembarkation, and the connection with the American coast lines, will effect a saving in time, as compared with the Panama route, of no less than five days between the Atlantic and Pacific ports of the United States.

"The Line will afford the easiest, safest, and speediest route between Great Britain and British Columbia; it will also afford the increased facilities of first-class ports for the establishment of speedy intercourse with Australia and New Zealand, and will bring Jamaica, Belize, and other British possessions in the West Indies, into the direct line of communication.

"Last year the dividend paid by the Panama Company was at the rate of 24 per cent. per annum on a capital of £1,600,000, in addition to a Bonus of 40 per cent. from accumulated profits. The Honduras Line will, in all probability, return as much profit as the Panama Line, if not considerably more.

"Sufficient of the proceeds of the present issue will be applied to the construction of the first section, from Puerto Caballos to Santiago. This section will enable the exportation of the mahogany, &c., to take place, the means of transport now existing being too expensive to be remunerative. Careful estimates have satisfied the Honduras Government that the surplus revenue of the State Domains and Forests will be amply sufficient to complete the whole Line, without any further issue of Stock; but in case it should be found advantageous, on account of increasing traffic, to accelerate the opening of the Railway from sea to sea, by raising more money, further Stock will be issued for the construction of the remaining sections of the Railway.

"The several contracts and other documents can be inspected at the Office of Messrs. Baxter, Rose, Norton, and Co., Solicitors, No. 6, Victoria Street, Westminster.

"Applications for the Loan will be received from Monday, 11th November, to Friday, the 15th November, by the London and County Bank, 21, Lombard Street, and Branches, where Prospectuses and Forms of Application can be obtained; and in Paris, by Messrs. Bischoffsheim, Goldschmidt, and Co., 26, Rue de la Chaussée d'Antin. Payments on application for the Loan can also be made at the Bank of France and Branches."

It may be seen, by the conditions of the foregoing Prospectus, that if the whole of the loan had been subscribed for at the price of issue, the nominal £1,000,000 would have produced on the 1st of April, 1869 (the date of the last instalment), the available sum of £735,937, from which sum the commission on the negotiation, and all the expenses, would then have to be deducted.

But that did not happen. The first Honduras loan, in spite of all the advantages which it offered to the subscribers, and the high respectability of the house which managed the operation, was received by the public with perfect indifference, with profound contempt; and according to the deficient and vague information which reached the Legation, there were hardly any other subscriptions than one of about £10,000 made by the firm of Bischoffsheim itself.

As soon as a loan is introduced to the public, it is necessary to obtain the official quotation of its bonds on 'Change; that is, the permission of the Directors of the Exchange for buying and selling the said bonds therein, with the privileges which they have in such cases. If the subscription has not been entirely filled up, and the official quotation is obtained, the sale of the bonds may go on subsequently by degrees, according to the price at which they are quoted in the market.

This latter was what happened to the Honduras loan of 1867. The expenses of introducing it to the public having been already incurred, and they are always very considerable, the contractors of the said loan, seeing the failure of the subscription, determined to go on with the sale of the bonds little by little on 'Change. But for this it was necessary that the public should see that the works of the Railway were commenced, that Engineers had already been sent out for that purpose, and that everything manifested a fixed determination to proceed with the work. For this purpose a sum of at least £40,000 was required, and this sum was advanced by Mr. Routelidge, Shipbroker, on receiving bonds of the said loan as security, and moreover the signature of the Minister himself.

A Committee of Trustees of the Honduras Government had already been appointed to administer the funds produced by the aforesaid loan, and it was composed of Messrs. Philip Thomas Blythe, William Henry Cotterell, Henry Luke Robinson, and Charles Lefèvre; and these Trustees were able to send

Mr. MacCandlish, and other Engineers to Honduras, to begin the works of the Railway with the small sum of money collected. By giving publicity to the commencement of the works, some confidence was imparted in regard to the undertaking, and a few bonds began to be sold.

But this sale was tardy, and it was necessary to accept prices much below that of the issue of the bonds, on account of the commission which had to be paid for negotiating them, and because the very fact of offering those bonds for sale in the market continually depreciated the price of quotation, in spite of all the prudence displayed in regard to the failure of the subscription on issuing them.

With the first proceeds of these sales it was necessary to meet some urgent payments; chiefly for the interest and redemption of the compounded Federal debt, which had to be paid every six months; then the £40,000 advanced by Routelidge, which it was needful to return; and again the funds which had been promised to the Government to enable it to provide for pressing internal requirements, and to maintain peace in the Republic; and lastly, what remained, to meet expenses of administration, and to attend to the construction of the Railway.

It will be easily understood that the operation of converting the bonds of the aforesaid loan into money on 'Change was necessarily very slow; and besides, the net produce of the sale of those bonds, after deducting commission and depreciation in the market, and providing for urgent requirements unconnected with the construction of the Railway, left but very little to meet the regular instalments which had to be paid to Messrs. Waring Brothers and MacCandlish, the contractors for the construction of the Line.

In the first contract of loan with Messrs. Bischoffsheim and Goldschmidt, it had been stipulated as a condition, that no other loan should in future be issued for the Railway, unless it were likewise contracted for and issued to the public by the firm of Messrs. Bischoffsheim and Goldschmidt; and in fact no one could appreciate the opportunity and the circumstances for having recourse to a fresh operation for the Railway so well as that firm, which knew the secrets of the results of the first loan, and was acquainted with the sacrifices which were still incurred in placing the bonds of that first loan; but this prudent clause, which concentred the responsibility of final success in the firm of Messrs. Bischoffsheim and Goldschmidt, was unfortunately destined to be without effect.

IV.

HONDURAS LOAN OF 207,509 BONDS OF 300 FRANCS EACH.—PARIS, 1869

SOME months after the issue of the first loan to the public, the Minister of Honduras at Paris, M. Herran, in concurrence with Sr D. Leon Alvarado, began to take steps for contracting a loan for the Honduras Railway in France, with the firm of Messrs. Dreyfus, Scheyer, & Co., on the ground that the loan issued in London had turned out a complete failure, and the proceeds of the bonds which were sold on 'Change were not sufficient to provide for the increasing requirements of the Railway and the interest of the loan itself. Messrs. Dreyfus, Scheyer, & Co. offered the Minister at Paris to put the said loan on the market, to the amount of 62,252,700 francs, divided into 207,509 bonds of 300 francs nominal value each; and they engaged to subscribe themselves for a third part, of course at a price much below that of issue.

The issue of this loan was contrary to the agreement made on starting the first loan with the firm of Bischoffsheim and Goldschmidt; and as the London firm refused to have anything to do in regard to the loan with the Paris firm that was bringing it out, there was a very serious quarrel between the houses of Bischoffsheim and Dreyfus, Scheyer, & Co., and with the Minister Herran. But the latter took such pains to carry out the affair, and the contentions arising from the opposition of Bischoffsheim and Goldschmidt threatened such serious complications, that the London house at last consented to the operation, though with dislike and apprehension of the result.

There had also been disagreements between the Trustees of the Government, as almost always happens when there is a diversity of opinion on difficult and complicated matters. One of the Trustees was dead, and the others did not want to remain; so it was necessary to appoint another new Committee in London, and the members of it were Messrs. Barnes, S. Davids, and Charles Lefèvre.

At the time when the second Honduras loan was about to be issued in France, which was in May, 1869, only a small portion of the first loan had been realized in England, which had not produced much more than a hundred thousand pounds in cash, the remaining bonds being in possession of the Trustees. This was the state of affairs when the Prospectus of the French loan appeared. The following is a translation of it.

"INTER-OCEANIC RAILWAY CONNECTING THE ATLANTIC WITH THE PACIFIC.

"*Secured Loan to the Government of Honduras (Central America).*

"Subscription, 207,509 Bonds.

"Price of the bonds 225 francs, payable as follows:

25 francs	on subscription,		With the right of paying one or more of these instalments in advance, and receiving a discount at the rate of 6 per cent. per annum.
50	,,	allotment	
50	,,	1 June (1869),	
50	,,	1 July ,,	
50	,,	1 August ,,	

"*Returns.—Repayment.—Participating Shares.*

"INTEREST.—Twenty francs a year, paid half-yearly on the 1st of March and the 1st of September, at Paris, Brussels, Antwerp, Geneva, in cash without any tax or deduction, and also at Berlin, Hamburg, Amsterdam, Frankfort, Genoa, New York, at the rate of the day. The first coupon is due on the 1st of September next.

"REPAYMENT.—At par in seventeen years by half-yearly drawings before a Notary at Paris; the first drawing will take place on the 1st of August next. The bonds drawn will be paid in cash on the 1st of September, *without any tax or deduction whatever.*

"PARTICIPATING SHARES.—Each bond will be replaced as soon as it is drawn by a PARTICIPATING SHARE, which will entitle the owner, after the repayment of the Loan, and during a period of fifteen years, to a proportional share in the third part of the revenues of the Line.

"This participation is estimated by the engineers at a minimum of 50 francs per annum.

"As the periods of the different payments and profits since the first of March last reduce the price of the subscription to about 220 *francs,* the produce of the debentures,* taking into consideration the premium of repayment, exceeds 12 *per cent.,* without reckoning the value of the *Participating Share.*

"*Guarantees for the Debentures.*

"(*a.*) MORTGAGE on the Railway and on ITS REVENUES.

"(*b.*) MORTGAGE on the domains and forests OF THE STATE, of which the annual revenue, according to the official report of the engineers, amply exceeds the sum necessary for the regular payment of interest and redemption.

"(*c.*) Convinced of the commercial and political importance of the Inter-oceanic Honduras Railway, the Governments of France, England, and the United States have, by international treaties, specially guaranteed the inviolability and neutrality of the undertaking, from the opening of the Line.

"(*d.*) A Commission has been appointed to superintend the employment of the Loan, which is to be exclusively devoted to the completion of the Line already in process of construction.

---

* The nominal value of the bonds of the French loan was 300 francs each. The prospectus does not mention this, nor does it give the total amount of the loan, which was 62,252,700 francs, or £2,490,108.

" This commission is composed of :
>
> His Excellency, M. V. Herran, Officer of the Legion of Honour, President (O. ✠) ; and
>
> MM. L. Pelletier, Chevalier of the Legion of Honour, an eminent merchant (C. ✠).
>
> R. Bischoffsheim.
>
> M. Scheyer.

" (e.) The execution of the Line is entrusted, by contract, to Messrs. Waring Brothers and MacCandlish, of London.

>   " Distances from New York to San Francisco—
>
> " By way of Panama . . . 9,730 kilomètres.
>   ,,   Honduras . . . 8,074 kilomètres.
>
> "Thus the Honduras route saves   1,656 kilomètres.

" The proceeds of the Panama Line are well known. The annual traffic is about 200,000 passengers, and merchandise valued at over a thousand million francs.

" (f.) The statement of the Sinking Fund of the Loan, the Reports of the Engineers, the International Treaties, are deposited in the Chancellor's Office of the Legation, Rue de la Chaussée d'Antin, where the public may inspect them.

> " V^{or} HERRAN,
> " Minister Plenipotentiary of Honduras.

" The subscription will be open on Wednesday the 19th, to Friday the 28th of May, from eight in the morning until five in the evening, in the following towns :

" PARIS.—At the Chancellor's Office of the Legation, and of the Consulate General of Honduras, 10 Rue de la Chaussée d'Antin; at Messrs. Dreyfus, Scheyer, and Co., Government bankers, Rue de la Grange Batelière 16.

" Subscriptions may be paid at all the branches of the Bank of France, at the Provincial bankers mentioned in the local journals, where the Government has deposited the provisional and definitive shares of the Loan.

" The subscription will also be opened at BRUSSELS, HANOVER, BERLIN, HAMBURG, AMSTERDAM.

" Subscribers who wish to pay up beforehand may send at once the whole sum, 223 frs. 90 c. per share, less discount, and the definitive shares will be delivered or sent to them.

"After the subscription is completed, even if before the 25th of May, no fresh subscription will be taken."

This loan was coldly received at Paris; but it had an extraordinary effect upon the quotation of the bonds of the first loan. The public had noted a circumstance which was not likely to escape its penetration. The Minister of Honduras at Paris had issued to the public of France a loan of twice-and-a-half the amount of that issued in London, and without the co-operation of the firm of Bischoffsheim of London, which the agreement required; and moreover, the security given in London for the first loan was again charged with the French loan. The English public, already interested in the first loan, looked with suspicion on this conduct; and the complications, difficulties, and distrust increased. The bonds, which the Trustees had in their portfolios in London, went off very slowly, and at continually diminishing prices. The debentures of the Paris loan, which had not been subscribed for by the public, had to be converted, like those of the London loan, by selling them on account of the Government, for there was no means of placing them then. And this is the reason:—

Messrs. Dreyfus, Scheyer, and Co., the contractors for the French loan, had engaged with the Minister Herran to take on their own account, little more or less, a third part of the loan, that is, 65,279 bonds of 300 francs each, the nominal value of which was 19,583,700 francs. At the price of issue, at which they were offered to the public, that is, 225 francs each, they ought to have produced 14,687,775 francs; but, by their contract, Messrs. Dreyfus, Scheyer, and Co. took them at a price somewhat below 175 francs, as they were to pay the sum of 11,422,815 francs for them, from which there were various deductions still to be made. If the public subscribed for a third part of the loan, it is clear that such subscription only served to absorb the bonds taken by the firm of Dreyfus, Scheyer, and Co., and to give that house a profit of 3,264,960 francs, the difference between the price of subscription for the public and the price at which the said firm took them. If the public did not subscribe for the whole of the aforesaid third part, it is evident that the firm of Dreyfus, Scheyer, and Co. could not sell on 'Change the bonds which were still unplaced of the third part which it had taken; no bond could be sold on account of the Government from the two third parts which the firm of Dreyfus, Scheyer, and Co. had not taken, for the sale of those bonds could, according to the contract, only take place through them.

And so it happened. The French public did not subscribe for the third part of the shares taken by the firm of Dreyfus, Scheyer, and Co.; and the bonds which they sold on 'Change were, very naturally, taken from the remainder of the 65,279 bonds which were still in their possession.

Here is the result which the Government obtained from this operation, according to a memorandum of the transactions presented by the firm of Dreyfus, Scheyer, and Co. itself:—

Dr.—The Government Bankers, Messrs. Dreyfus, Scheyer, and Co., Paris.

	Francs. c.
The bankers have received 65,279 bonds of the Honduras loan in France, for which, according to agreement, and including interest, they owe	11,422,815/63
Bonus on coining money, according to contract between the Director of the Imperial Mint at Paris and M. Herran, the Minister Plenipotentiary	70,000/00
Total Dr. . . frs.	11,492,815/63

Cr.—The said Bankers, who have paid as follows:—

	Francs. c.
Expenses of printing the bonds, and for a globe for drawing the bonds for redemption	70,519/88
Carried over . . .	70,519/88

	Francs. c.
Brought over . . .	70,519/18
Service of coupons and redemption, Nos. 1 and 2, including commission	1,062,136/20
Agreement of 25th February, 1869, for coining nickel money, representing 5,000,000 francs . . .	3,000,000/00
Payments made for commission at Paris, and for the Minister Herran, to Messrs. Waring, Brothers, and Co., and to Messrs. Bischoffsheim and Goldschmidt	4,481,392/95
Payments of indemnification, according to the agreement in London, 2nd July, 1870	2,307,500/00
Various payments to the Minister Herran, according to receipts .	571,266/60
The same amount . . . frs.	11,492,815/63

So that the result of the operation of the French Loan was a subscription by the firm of Dreyfus, Scheyer, and Co., for a third part of the whole loan, that is, a nominal sum of 19,583,700 francs—which only produced, for direct application to the Railway, the sum of 4,481,392 francs, from which is still to be deducted the sum paid to Messrs. Bischoffsheim and Goldschmidt for a different purpose not stated in this *Memorandum* of the account. For the rest, it is apparent at the first glance that the Committee appointed at Paris to superintend the employment of the proceeds of the loan, which, as is shown by the Prospectus, was to serve exclusively for the completion of the Line, diverted the sum of 3,000,000 francs for the purpose of coining money, representing 5,000,000 francs, which the Honduras Government was to put into circulation, and the intrinsic value of which did not much exceed a tenth part, that is, 500,000 francs.

Meanwhile the Government had in its possession the 142,230 bonds still unplaced, each for 300 francs nominal value, which, in proportion as their sale was forced on 'Change, would go on decreasing in value, until they came down to the ruinous price of 20 francs per bond, as it actually happened.

Messrs. Bischoffsheim and Goldschmidt of London were so much displeased, that the greatest efforts on the part of the Minister in London were required to prevent them from carrying out their intention of throwing up the affair altogether, which would have caused the complete ruin of the Railway and the loss of all hope for Honduras.

At this time great and terrible events were brewing in Europe. No one could have expected that they would produce the lamentable effects which they did produce, or that they were to disturb all operations upon 'Change, and exercise a pernicious and paralysing influence upon all enterprises founded on credit.

The Minister in London had duly reported to the Supreme Government on the result of the loan in Paris, on the new complications which had arisen, and the unbearable state of affairs, if fresh resources were not in some way sought for.

The million dollars in nickel coin, or 5,000,000 francs, the manufacture of which cost 3,000,000 francs, abstracted from the French loan, was of no use at all to the Government, because the Honduras public would not accept its circulation; and the Government, having no other resource at disposal for the construction of the Railway, was obliged to try that expedient again, which had already produced such evil results twice over, that is, a third loan, in order to see whether the completion of the Railway, the object of all its aspirations, could be effected by that means. Accordingly the Government sent over fresh powers to contract that third loan: they bear date the 14th of March, 1870.

V.

HONDURAS LOAN OF TWO MILLION FIVE HUNDRED THOUSAND POUNDS.—LONDON, 1870.

It is easy to understand the difficulty of issuing a third loan for the construction of the Honduras Railway, when there were already two in the market, one in London and the other at Paris—the public being alarmed at the conditions of the second loan, and the Government having no new guarantees to offer, either real or even nominal.

Various considerable sums had been sent to the Honduras Government, not only for the purpose of providing for its peremptory internal requirements, but also to proceed with the cutting and exportation of mahogany, and the working of some mines, for the purpose of remitting the produce to Europe and thereby attracting public attention. But the Government was unable to send either mahogany or metals; and only after much exertion was the arrival in Europe announced of two cargoes of mahogany on account of the Honduras Government, of which the news alone produced the best effects. Unfortunately that mahogany had not been cut and prepared by order of the Honduras Government; it had been bought by the Government from the mahogany merchants on the North coast, and when it came to Europe was found to be of the most inferior quality, and much of it in bad condition.

There was also a cargo of timber which came direct from Amapala, besides those which the Government sent from Belize.

Finally, it was determined to put the third Honduras loan for the completion of the Railway on the market, as the only available resource for meeting the engagements with the Contractors for the Line, and others, which were pending.

The prospectus of this third loan appeared on the 20th June, 1870. It was as follows:—

"1870.

"HONDURAS TEN PER CENT. GOVERNMENT RAILWAY LOAN.

"£2,500,000.

"*In 25,000 Bonds of £100 each, bearing 10 per cent. Annual Interest, payable half-yearly, viz., on 1st January and 1st July.*

"Issued at 80 per cent., and to be redeemed at par, in sterling, within 15 years, by Yearly Drawings, on the 31st December in each year, by means of an Accumulative Sinking Fund of 3 per cent. per annum.

"The first Drawing to take place on the 31st December, 1870.

"The instalments to be paid as follows :—

15 per cent. on Allotment.
10 per cent. on 1st August.
10 per cent. on 1st September.
15 per cent. on 1st October.
15 per cent. on 1st November.
15 per cent. on 15th December, when definitive Bonds, with a Coupon of £5 payable on the 1st January attached, will be given in exchange for scrip.

---

80 per cent.

"Interest will date from the 1st July.

"The instalments may be anticipated at any time when an instalment falls due, under discount at the Bank of England rate.

"PROSPECTUS.

"His Excellency Señor Don Carlos Gutierrez, Minister Plenipotentiary of the Government of the Republic of Honduras to the Court of St. James's, being authorized by full powers, dated 14th March, 1870, to raise for his Government a Loan of Two Millions sterling net, for the completion from sea to sea of the Inter-oceanic Honduras Railway, has instructed the London and County Bank to receive applications for the same.

"The Loan will be represented by Bonds to bearer of £100 each, bearing interest, until redeemed, at the rate of 10 per cent. per annum, payable half-yearly on the 1st January and 1st July in each year, at the London and County Bank.

"The whole Loan will be redeemed within 15 years by an

accumulative Sinking Fund of 3 per cent. per annum, to be applied by annual drawings, the said drawings to take place on the 31st December in each year, in the presence of the Honduras Minister in London, a representative of Messrs. Bischoffsheim and Goldschmidt, and a Notary Public, and the Bonds so drawn will be paid within one month thereafter.

"This Loan is raised to complete the Inter-oceanic Railway, and to place the Line from sea to sea in thorough and efficient working order. As in the case of the previous Loan, the proceeds of the present Loan will be paid into the hands of Trustees appointed for that purpose.

"The entire Railway and its revenue is mortgaged to the Bondholders of all denominations, and the proceeds of the State domains will be applied in a like manner.

"The first section is contracted to be finished next November. Messrs. Waring Brothers and M'Candlish have undertaken, under heavy penalty, to complete the second section at the end of 1871; and a new contract has been signed with them to complete the entire Railway from Puerto Caballos, on the Atlantic coast, to the Bay of Fonseca, on the Pacific, and to deliver it over in efficient working order in the autumn of 1872.

"The Railway is under the protection of the British Government by a treaty, which declares:—

'In order to secure the construction and permanence of the route or road herein contemplated, and also to secure for the benefit of mankind the uninterrupted advantages of such communication from sea to sea, Her Britannic Majesty recognizes the rights of Sovereignty and property of Honduras in and over the line of the said road, and for the same reason guarantees, positively and efficaciously, the entire neutrality of the same. And when the proposed road shall have been completed, Her Britannic Majesty equally engages, in conjunction with the Republic of Honduras, to protect the same from interruption, seizure, or unjust confiscation, from whatsoever quarter the attempt may proceed.'

"Treaties signed by the Honduras Government with France and the United States contain the same provisions.

"A general Bond, executed by His Excellency Don Carlos Gutierrez on behalf of the Government of Honduras, will be deposited at the Bank of England for security of the entire Loan, and the Definitive Bonds of this Loan will be signed by His

Excellency Don Carlos Gutierrez, on behalf of his Government, and countersigned by Messrs. Bischoffsheim and Goldschmidt, agents of the Government in England.

"Applications for the Loan will be received by the London and County Bank, 21, Lombard Street, and Branches, where Prospectuses and Forms of Application can be obtained.

"London, June 20th, 1870."

At the same time a third Committee of Trustees was appointed, composed of Messrs. Ford, Widdicombe, and Blythe, in whom Messrs. Bischoffsheim and Goldschmidt fully confided, and of Mr. Charles Lefèvre.

This Committee undertook to receive the accounts of its predecessors in London, and also to receive the bonds of the Paris loan which were still unsold.

The new loan had been prepared with the utmost care, and without sparing any necessary expense, in order to ensure its success. Both on 'Change and in the Press there was a multitude of persons who supported the operation; and the English public, already the most interested in the completion of the Railway, met this loan with a satisfactory subscription. For a moment the operation was assured, and there was a possibility of finishing the Railway by this means. But only a few days after the distribution of the subscription, the Franco-Prussian war broke out, with its hostilities, defeats, and catastrophes, causing a most frightful depreciation of all funds. There seemed to be a fatality against the success of every operation for the termination of the Honduras Railway.

It was necessary to employ the scrip of this loan, which represented the 15 per cent., corresponding with the first instalment, in purchasing bonds, in order to prevent an alarming or ruinous fall which would ruin the operation; and the trustees had to do with three loans in the market, that of 1867, still not fully realized; that of 1869, of which two-thirds were unplaced; and that of 1870, the bonds of which were all in possession of the Trustees, and the sale of them on 'Change could only be commenced after the 15th of December.

On the other hand, the engagements contracted were becoming more and more pressing; the interest and redemption fund of the Federal debt had to be paid every six months; the interest and redemption fund of that part of the London loan of 1867, and of the Paris loan of 1869, which had been placed, had also to be discharged every six months ; it was necessary to pay off the offers made to the Government to assist it with considerable sums for the purpose of preserving internal order, and the Government drew on the Trustees on account of the sums offered; and, lastly, it was necessary to pay the contractors Messrs. Waring Brothers and MacCandlish the instalments which were due to them from time to time for carrying on the works. If any of these payments should be neglected, the consequences would be fatal.

It was quite impossible to dispose on 'Change of the number of bonds required to meet these engagements as speedily as they were accumulating. Any public offer for the sale of twenty or thirty thousand pounds' worth of bonds would produce an enormous fall in the prices of quotation; so that it was most important not to alarm the market, in order to maintain the quotation price as high as possible. But as time went on, and the engagements became due from day to day, there was no resource but to employ the expedient of selling the bonds to the speculators on 'Change, at a much lower rate than the price of quotation, in order that they should advance the money most needed, and should place the bonds in the market, on their own account, by degrees and without causing alarm.

The risk and difficulty of this operation for those who took bonds on their own account, and the price at which it was necessary to dispose of the bonds to induce them to incur that risk, will be easily understood ; and even thus it was difficult to find those who would take enough to get rid once more of the pending engagements.

The result of all this appears to be, from a careful and very approximate calculation, that the £5,990,108, to which the three loans of 1867, 1870, and 1871 amount, hardly produced, upon an average, an available 45 per cent. on their nominal value, that is, some £2,695,000.

The application of this sum may, in *approximate figures*, be divided as follows:—

Interest and redemption paid for these loans, and for the Federal debt up to March 1, 1873, the date of last payment of interest on the French loan	£1,100,000
Coining the nickel money	120,000
For the construction of the first section of the Railway, and materials for the second and third sections	1,050,000
Various sums placed at the disposal of the Government, or paid on its account, including old debts of the Government paid in London, bills accepted and paid, consignments of arms, money paid for working mines, &c.	180,000
Salary and commission paid to the Government engineer, pay of the trustees, commission, general expenses, &c. &c.	245,000
	£2,695,000

Before concluding the history of the Honduras loans, it was necessary to introduce the approximate figures of their produce, because they show clearly what must have been the confusion amongst the persons who conducted those operations, when they found their efforts to improve a situation s painful, so unavoidable, and so serious, frustrated on all sides. In the middle of the year 1871, in spite of all the efforts and sacrifices made to place the bonds and debentures of the three contracted loans, there were still unplaced bonds to the amount of £2,000,000 nominal value. Even if this sum had been realized as the rest was realized, not only would it have been insufficient to complete the construction of half the Line, but it would hardly have covered the interest and redemption of the said loans up to the end of the year 1872. Then the Engineer of the Honduras Government, Mr. James Brunlees, one of the most eminent and accredited in England, supported by the no less eminent Engineer, Edward Woods, President of the Society of Civil Engineers, suggested to the contractors for the loans in London, to the Trustees, and to the Honduras Government itself, the idea of converting the projected Interoceanic Railway into a triple line railway, that might transport vessels up to a thousand tons' burthen and their cargoes from sea to sea, on special trucks; a gigantic, colossal, bold idea, which, though not new, was of universal interest, if practicable; and its practicability was scientifically discussed and proved, and could not be doubted by the public in general, when it came from two such eminent Engineers as Brunlees and Woods, and in an age which has seen electric cables stretched across the ocean, a passage for ships opened between the Mediterranean and the Red Sea across the Isthmus of Suez, locomotives traversing the Alps after the perforation of an immense tunnel in Mount Cenis, and works prepared for opening another tunnel from England to France under the Channel.

The Contractors for the loans in London were enthusiastically in favour of the idea, and conceived a financial combination to present the project to the public. That combination was, at least, to produce the conclusion of the interoceanic road already begun, and thus get over the difficulties which surrounded the enterprise.

VI.

PROJECT FOR CONVERTING THE RAILWAY ACROSS HONDURAS INTO AN INTER-OCEANIC RAILWAY TO TRANSPORT SHIPS.

THE calculations of the profits which a Railway across Honduras must produce are so satisfactory and flattering that, according to them, from the moment when that Line can be finished and opened for traffic, one of the principal causes will disappear which have rendered the sacrifices made in the loans useless; and it has been and is that which bars the success of every combination based upon credit to re-establish confidence and give new life to the undertaking. Were the Line once completed, the profits which its working would produce, the value which the uncultivated lands on each side of the line would acquire, the exportation of the timber from the extensive forests which it traverses, and the mines in the vicinity of the Line, well managed, would be more than sufficient to make satisfactory arrangements with the bond-holders, and to reduce the debt nominally contracted to equitable terms, in exchange for the assurance which those elements duly managed would afford for the payment of the interest.

Hence the anxiety of those in favour of or interested in this enterprise to finish the Line at all events, convinced that when once it is finished it will itself produce sufficient to clear off all liabilities incurred.

When the project for converting the Line into a Ship-railway was laid before the public, it was hoped that the idea would be sufficiently supported to afford means for finishing provisionally the Line already begun; and afterwards, according as the enthusiasm of the public was displayed, to go on with the works for converting the Line into a Ship-railway, or to abandon the project.

The same idea of constructing a Railway to transport vessels across Central America had been communicated to the Government of the Republic of Costa Rica as practicable for that country, and the measures for its acceptance by that Republic were considerably advanced, on the terms which Mr. Lefèvre had proposed to the Minister for Foreign Affairs.

The Supreme Government of Honduras, which was fully aware of all the mischances met with in the previous loans, and the insuperable accumulated difficulties in providing the funds to proceed with the Line already begun, and to obtain half-yearly the enormous sums required to pay the interest and redemption of the loans, determined to accept the new idea of soliciting from the public another loan to convert the Railway in course of construction into a Ship-railway, and sent over special powers to carry it out; they bear date the 24th of November, 1871.

The Minister in London distrusted the success of the operation, not only on account of the difficulties which he supposed there would be in effecting it, but also an account of the enormous sum which it was necessary to ask from the public for the purpose, and on account of the sad lesson taught by the previous attempts.*

But the Minister in London could not take upon himself the responsibility of opposing what was proposed by the eminent Engineers who were in the service of Honduras, and the Contractors for the loans, above all when the latter

---

* The Minister in London only received a private report from a Spanish Engineer, adverse to the project of the Ship-railway, which had no weight against the opinion of two Engineers so eminent as Brunlees and Woods. "That work," said the report, "though practicable in theory, is immensely difficult in practice, amongst other reasons, on account of the stupendous radius with which it is necessary to trace the Line. If fifteen or twenty millions are placed at the disposal of the Engineers, perhaps they may overcome the difficulties; but even then it is problematical whether the results would correspond with such enormous expenses." There are, however, very respectable Engineers who are still enthusiastically in favour of a Ship-railway across Honduras or the Isthmus of Panama.

declared that it was impossible to finish the Line, or to go on paying the dividends of the interest on the loans; and besides, the Government had already accepted the project, and sent powers, orders, and instructions for the purpose.

The Minister in London tried all he could, consistently with his official character, to oppose the project, but it was in vain. The Trustees, the engineers, the contractors for the loans, Mr. Sharp, the legal adviser of the firm of Bishoffsheim, affirmed that it was an absolute necessity, and the only means of attaining a good result, to propose to the public the conversion of the Line into a Ship-railway, and to solicit as a loan the sum necessary for it.

On the other hand, the Contractors for the works already begun, Waring Brothers and MacCandlish, were continually threatening to suspend or abandon the works and give the matter up, unless they were paid what was due to them, and regularly received the instalments agreed upon in their contracts. Moreover, they had brought serious claims against the Government, demanding enormous damages for not having been paid in due time the stipulated sums for the construction of the Line, from which default of payment they alleged that they had already suffered ruinous losses.

In answer to the complaints of these gentlemen respecting irregularity of payment, they were blamed by the Honduras Government for not having performed the works of that part of the Line already constructed so substantially and properly as was required; but the Trustees of the Government were not in a position to proceed against those contractors energetically, because they were in their hands; and in order to avoid worse evils and judicial proceedings, they determined, in concurrence with the contractors for the loan in London, to revoke the contract with Messrs. Waring Brothers and MacCandlish, and to entrust the execution of the work to other Engineers who would be less pressing for the money required for the construction, and more scrupulous in duly executing the works. For this purpose an agreement was made with the said contracting Engineers, revoking the contract for construction on payment of what was due to them up to that date.

On the 22nd of May, 1872, then, the project was issued to the public,* explaining the theory of the conversion of the Line into a Ship-railway, its practicability, the difficulties which stood in its way, and the means of overcoming them, as well as the advantages which might accrue to maritime commerce by relieving vessels bound from the Atlantic to the Pacific Ocean from the difficult and long navigation by Cape Horn or the Straits of Magellan. To carry out this gigantic enterprise, a loan of £15,000,000 was demanded from the public.

Messrs. Bischoffsheim of London were to sign the bonds which should be issued for this loan; and, in concurrence with them, the operation was conducted by Mr. Charles Lefèvre and the legal adviser of Messrs. Bischoffsheim, Mr. Sharp, in whose possession were deposited all the documents relative to this operation, in order that the public might examine them, and he was the solicitor who prepared and drew up all the contracts necessary for the purpose.

For greater precaution, Captain Bedford Pim was provisionally appointed as Special Commissioner of the Government of Honduras, for the purpose of watching over the interests of the Government; and this gentleman was selected because he was perfectly well acquainted with the Republic of Honduras, and the affairs of the Railway, as well as because he was greatly esteemed in London for his activity, understanding, and previous conduct.

Five days after the project was presented to the public the news arrived in London of the revolution in Honduras, the invasion of its territory by the forces of Guatemala and Salvador, and the defeat and deposition of the President of the

---

* See Appendix, No. V.

Republic, General Medina. This news caused an immediate fall of 40 per cent. in the quoted price of the Honduras loans, which at cost of great sacrifices had been raised to 70 per cent.

Then the Committee of Foreign Bondholders informed those who were conducting the operation, that the announcement of the new loan solicited for the construction of the Ship-railway would be opposed; and, in consideration of such serious antagonism, the said loan was prudently withdrawn from the market, fortunately without the Government having to pay the expenses incurred in organizing it.

The six months for the payment of the interest and redemption fund of the three loans already contracted, were about to expire, and it was necessary to announce their proximate payment, so that the value of the bonds should rise again, and to show at the same time that the Honduras revolution did not in any way affect the Railway undertaking. It was also necessary, at all events, to come to an accommodation with the contractors for the Line, Waring Brothers and MacCandlish, so that, notwithstanding the revocation of the contract, they should go on with the works of the Railway, which they would not do without more money.

The prospects of obtaining that money were very gloomy, and yet it was absolutely necessary to obtain it at any sacrifice, not only because, if the payment of the interest and redemption of the loans were not announced, and if the Railway works did not go on, everything would be ruined, but also because this was the sole means of gaining time to inform the new Government of all that had occurred, and to ask it for decisive instructions.

With this object in view, the aforesaid Mr. Charles Lefèvre advanced a sufficient sum to meet those urgent necessities, and it was deposited at a bank; then the public was informed at once through the newspapers that the funds for the payment of the interest and redemption of the three loans for the current half-year were ready and deposited in the bank.

Mr. Charles Lefèvre received in exchange for the sum advanced an equivalent amount in bonds at the price quoted on 'Change, and it was left to him to realise those bonds when he pleased.

VII.

MISSION OF A COMMISSIONER TO HONDURAS TO REPORT TO THE PROVISIONAL GOVERNMENT.—ANOTHER LOAN PROJECTED AT PARIS.

In concurrence with the Trustees and the Contractors for the loans in England, the Minister in London determined to send out a commissioner to Honduras to inform the Government of the Provisional President, Señor Don Céleo Arias, of the real state of affairs, then to propose to the Government some urgent arrangements, to recommend certain projects and plans which might save the Railway undertaking from a total collapse, and, above all, to request precise and detailed instructions as to what was to be done.

Another half-year's interest and redemption of the English loans would become due on the 1st of January, 1873; and as the Trustees had not sufficient funds, either in ready money or in bonds for sale, to meet those payments, it was absolutely necessary that the new Government should give the necessary directions to get out of these miserable difficulties in some way or other, so that there might be time to carry them out before those engagements became due. D. Ramon de Silva Ferro, the Secretary of the Legation in London, was charged with this delicate mission; he left Southampton for Honduras on the 17th of July, 1872, and he was to return with instructions to London before the following December.

The Secretary, Señor de Silva Ferro, reached Comayagua, the capital of the Republic, on the 22nd of August, 1872; and he at once presented to the Government a circumstantial report, giving an exact account of the very serious state of the Railway affairs and of those of its loans. The Secretary took with him, for delivery to the Government, the accounts presented by the firm of Dreyfus, Scheyer, and Co., respecting the French loan; the current account of the Trustees in London; all the reports and previous proceedings, to aid the Government in the examination of those accounts; a project for the concession of uncultivated lands on each side of the Railway, to offer them to the bond-holders as a special guarantee, by means of which the revocation of the general and abstract pledge made for the loans was to be proposed, which extends to all the uncultivated lands and forests of the Republic, and a suitable arrangement was to be offered to the bond-holders, so that the construction of the Railway might be carried on with ease. He likewise took out a project for a "Bank Concession," and also one for a "Mine Law," with some others of a partial character intended to promote the arrangement of the Railway affairs.

But the Government of the President, Señor Arias, which had just been established at Comayagua, had already formed a very different judgment of the state of the Railway affairs, and the causes of its mishaps. Public opinion charged the ex-President General Medina, then in solitary confinement in a prison at Comayagua, with having diverted from the loans contracted in Europe for the Railway many and enormous sums, which he had deposited, as it was said, in some European banks for his personal use; and the same accusation was made, with absurd exaggerations, against some other functionaries who had acted in the name of the Government. No one in Honduras had the least idea of the real causes of such *contretemps;* and all was explained in the most easy and simple manner, by assuming that the Government had collected about six millions sterling for the construction of the Railway, and that five-sixths of that sum, which belonged to the Republic, had stuck to the fingers of those who had the management of the business.

All the previous official proceedings, all the documents concerning the Railway and its loans, had disappeared, or had been destroyed, during the revolution; and the then President, Señor D. Céleo Arias, had already decided to appoint confidential Commissioners to investigate in Europe the truth of all that had occurred.

The exact statement of the facts, and the plain and truthful, though discouraging, picture of the state of these affairs in Europe, as presented to the Government by the Secretary of the Legation in the name of the Minister in London, made the Government aware of the seriousness of the circumstances, and the difficulty of prescribing efficient measures to remedy them.

The Government of Señor Arias then first understood the signification of the nominal figures which represented the contracted loans; the causes which had led to the failure of those loans, and reduced them to less than a moiety in cash.

The Government allowed about six weeks to elapse without coming to any apparent resolution, not even that of appointing a Committee to examine the documents brought by the Secretary sent from London. Then the latter solicited, in the name of the Minister in London, that a Special Commissioner in the confidence of the Government, a native of Honduras, and of known patriotism and honour, should be sent to England with sufficient power and authority to adopt the necessary measures in Europe; and for that purpose he suggested to the Government that it would be well to select Señor D. Ponciano Leiva, then Minister for Foreign Affairs, as most fitting to discharge such a delicate commission, by his civic merits and the public approbation which he had earned.

The President did not accede to this suggestion, but directed that Dr. C. E. Bernhard, German Consul at Amapala, and wholly in his confidence, should be authorized for the purpose, and be invested with ample powers to act as Commissioner in concurrence with the Minister in London.

M. Adolphe Herran, son of the Minister of Honduras at Paris, and attached to that Legation, was at Comayagua at the same time. His mission at Comayagua was to solicit, on the part of the Minister at Paris, the approval of the accounts of the French loan of 1869, presented by the firm of Dreyfus, Scheyer, and Co., and by the Minister himself; to re-validate his credentials as Minister, which had been withdrawn, in regard to Paris, by the previous President, General Medina, shortly before his fall; to obtain some directions from the Government concerning certain matters which the said Minister had in hand at Paris; and to make official reports to the Government respecting the events, from his own point of view. At the same time he tried to induce the President to contract a new loan through the said house of Dreyfus, Scheyer, and Co., for the purpose of meeting the pending difficulties, for which he said he had instructions and powers from Messrs. Dreyfus, Scheyer, and Co.

A few days before the Secretary of the Legation in London, and the appointed Financial Commissioner, Dr. C. E. Bernhard, left for Europe—the latter, with general powers to act in concurrence with the Minister in London, and with reserved powers to act independently, if he thought fit—the President, Señor Arias signed with M. Adolphe Herran, acting in the name of the firm of Dreyfus, Scheyer, and Co., a contract *ad referendum*, for a loan which those bankers undertook to raise for the completion of the Railway.

The conditions of that loan were so absurd, considering the complicated state of Honduras affairs in Europe, and so prejudical to the firm of Dreyfus, Scheyer, and Co. itself, that the Secretary of the Legation in London pointed this out to the President in the presence of the Ministers, expressing doubts as to whether M. Adolphe Herran had instructions from Messrs. Dreyfus, Scheyer, and Co. to propose such a contract for loan on those terms. Nevertheless, the President, Señor Arias, had faith and hope in the operation contracted for, and

M. Adolphe Herran immediately started for Europe in order to arrive in November, and before the Secretary of the Legation in London and the Special Commissioner of the Government should be dispatched on the same voyage.

Besides the loan-contract with which M. Adolphe Herran returned to Paris, he had obtained for his father his restoration as Minister of Honduras at Paris, with instructions not to meddle with the financial affairs of the loans or the Railway.

The Secretary of the Legation in London, and the Commissioner appointed by the Government, were to leave for Europe a fortnight after M. Adolphe Herran had done so. But, unfortunately, the steamer which was to take them from the Bay of Fonseca to Panama, was wrecked on the coast, and the two travellers could not arrive in London before the end of December, 1872.

Meanwhile, there was no news in London of what the Government intended to do. The Trustees had resigned; the commercial house of M. Charles Lefèvre had closed, and its principal was gone to France; a new Committee o Trustees had been appointed, comprising Messrs. G. B. Kerferd, Edward Haslewood, and Captain Bedford Pim; the bonds of the Honduras loan had sunk until they were quoted from 20 to 25 per cent., and the loan-contract brought over by M. Adolphe Herran had been repudiated by Messrs. Dreyfus, Scheyer, and Co., of Paris.

All hope having vanished of obtaining instructions from the Government in sufficient time to make them effective, Captain Bedford Pim, acting provisionally as Commissioner of the Government of Honduras, and the Trustee Mr. G. B. Kerferd, both authorized by the Minister in London, determined to try another loan, which was to be asked for at Paris; it was to be £200,000, 10 per cent. stock.

This is the Prospectus:—

"Financial Agency of the Honduras Government, Paris.

"Issue of 5,000,000 francs (or £200,000) 10 per Cent. Stock.

"Repayable at par in seventeen years, dating from 1874.

"To be divided into shares of 20, 100, 500, 1000, 2500, 5000, 10,000 f.

"*Price of Issue.*

| 70 francs for every 100 francs Stock, payable | 10 francs on Application
10 ,, Allotment
15 ,, 15 February, 1873
15 ,, 15 April, 1873
20 ,, 15 June, 1873 | 70 francs, |

with the option of paying the whole at the time of subscription, with a discount of 6 per cent., or an allowance of one franc, which will reduce the net price to 69 francs.

"The option of discount will be withdrawn after the closing of the subscriptions.

"*Guarantees.*

"A. *The general disposable revenues of the State.*

"B. *A special appropriation* of the lands lying along the Interoceanic Railway now in course of construction, and of which the first section is already working. The lands, which will be registered in the names of the Trustees in London specially appointed by the Government, will be disposed of by the latter on leases for 99 years, to repay, if need be, even in anticipation, the shares of the present loan.

"The Honduras Government binds itself, in order to favour immigration, not to increase the price of the lands beyonds 50 piastres (250 francs) the manzana (¾ of a hectare), which is their lowest current price. The actual guarantee being 2 hectares to each 10 francs of Stock, the security is absolute.

"The above guarantees are specially mentioned in the *General Bond* deposited by the Honduras Government in the Bank of England.

"The product of the present Loan, after having provided for the completion of the Railway, for the purchase of material and machines, and for public works, will be applied to the foreign financial services of the Honduras Government.

Proceeds.—Sinking Fund.

"The *Interest will be paid* half-yearly at Paris, London, Hanover, Geneva, &c.

"The *first coupons* will be paid on the 1st of July, 1873.

"The *redemption* will take place in 17 years by half-yearly drawings and *equal annuities*. The first drawing will take place on the 1st of January, 1874.

"In proportion as the lands are disposed of by the Commissioners, more considerable repayments will be made in anticipation.

"The quotation on the Exchange at Paris will be demanded as soon as the issue is concluded.

"In conformity with the law of the 25th of May, 1872, declaration of the present issue was made on the 11th instant at the Registration and Stamp Office of the Seine, No. 790 *bis* of the register of the visa for stamping documents of Stocks and other public effects of foreign Governments. Consequently the shares issued in France will be delivered bearing the French stamp.

"BEDFORD PIM,
Special Commissioner of the
Honduras Government.

"*Paris, 15 December, 1872.*"

To inspire confidence in the money market of France with regard to this operation, the payment was announced of the interest of the 1869 loan, which became due on the 1st of April, for which purpose the necessary funds were deposited, derived from the bonds which remained in the possession of the Trustees in London. There was now nothing left to pay the interest and redemption of the English loans which fell due in January, and they could only be met in case the new loan attempted at Paris should turn out successful.

All was prepared by the middle of December, 1872, to put it on the market; then the Minister in Paris, M. Herran, and the Consul-General, M. Pelletier, protested against this operation on the 24th of December. This gave rise to the disputes and debates with Captain Bedford Pim, which have been extensively circulated by the " Foreign Times " of the 15th of January, 1873.

Dr. Bernhard, the Special Commissioner of the Honduras Government, and the Secretary of the Legation in London, Señor de Silva Ferro, arrived in London while these things were going on.

VIII.

MEETING OF THE HONDURAS BONDHOLDERS, ON THE 10th OF JANUARY, 1873.

A Meeting of the Honduras Bondholders was called by Captain Bedford Pim, R.N., the Special Commissioner of Honduras, to be held on the 6th inst.; but on account of the illness of Captain Pim, it was postponed to the 10th inst., at 2.30 p.m., at the London Tavern, Bishopsgate Street, where a crowded and important assemblage of the bondholders took place. The gallant Captain was so far recovered as to be able to take the chair exactly at the appointed time, and gave the meeting the very clear statement which we now publish in full detail.

Captain Bedford Pim, upon entering the room, was received with cheers, and after taking the chair proceeded to deliver the following speech:—

"GENTLEMEN,—I appear before you to-day to give an account of my stewardship as Special Commissioner of Honduras, and, in order to make my statement as clear as possible to every one, I shall divide what I have to say into two parts; the first comprising an account of the present actual position of Honduras and the bondholders; and the second, my individual participation in the events which have happened since our meeting in the summer of last year.

I can safely say that my bitter disappointment and grief at having to announce to you that neither coupon nor drawing is at present forthcoming is not second to that of any bondholder present; but that this misfortune has arisen in a manner nobody could have foreseen, will be abundantly proved to you presently.

The only comfort I can give you at present is the assurance that it has never entered the heads of those in authority in Honduras to repudiate their national debt. On the contrary, I can assert without fear of contradiction, that every exertion has been made to fulfil the financial obligations of the State, and complete the Inter-oceanic Railway, upon which the hopes of both natives and bondholders are so intimately bound up.

I firmly believe that every penny of the indebtedness of Honduras will be discharged if only time is given; and if I did not so believe,

I would not retain the appointment of Special Commissioner for one single moment. And here I feel it my duty to you, in proof of what I have just said, to inform you that all the loans have been raised for the sole purpose of building the Inter-oceanic Railway, and that, so far as I can understand figures, the Government of Honduras positively have used only the very smallest percentage of those loans for any other purpose but the Railway from 1867 to the present day, a period of five years. If any one wants a better proof of the singleness of purpose and honesty of the Honduras Government, I can only say he is very unreasonable.

Gentlemen, I have received letters without number from bondholders. I have not answered any of them, because I felt that I owed a duty to the general body, and not to individuals. Verbally, I have spared no pains during the last six months to afford every information to inquiring bondholders who have waited upon me personally. I make this statement, because I should be very sorry if any bondholder thought me unfeeling because I did not answer his letter. These letters from bondholders contain every sort of question bearing upon the matter now before us which it is possible to conceive; and I think it will, perhaps, be the wisest course for me to adopt, if I take those questions *seriatim,* and give a reply to each.

I need not say that, if any one has any other questions relevant to Honduras to ask, I shall gladly answer them.

The following are the questions I refer to :—

1.—Q. Can you state that the money of bondholders has been expended with judgment and due economy?

A. The money has been expended in the only possible way, viz.—

1.—In prosecuting the railway works so far as the internal dissensions of the country would permit.

2.—In providing the coupons and drawing of the bondholders.

2.—Q. Supposing the present Government to be upset, is there any succeeding Government likely to repudiate the existing debts, or to fail to pay dividends punctually?

A. Repudiation under any circumstances is most unlikely, as is proved by the consistent desire on the part of those in power, of all shades in politics, to finish the Inter-oceanic Railway.

3.—Q. Supposing there is money enough, and no political interruption, when do you expect the railway to be finished?

A. Within about two years.

4.—Q. Is there enough money to finish the railway?

A. Certainly not.

5.—Q. Are you a bondholder yourself?

A. Certainly not. I have never held a bond, and never made or lost a single shilling in Honduras stock.

6.—*Q.* Is there a prospect of peace in the country?

A. There is a fair prospect of peace in the country; but upon this point Dr. Bernhard, a commissioner, who has arrived within the last few days from Honduras, will be able to give you the latest information.

7.—*Q.* What has become of the difference between the amount realized on the sale of the bonds and the actual amount paid to the contractors for the railway?

A. I am sorry to say that the money referred to has been paid away in drawings and coupons, instead of being devoted to the purposes of the railway, during the valuable time lost in revolutions and the war between Salvador with Guatemala against Honduras.

8.—*Q.* What amount of money has been paid to the contractors of the railway on account of works?

A. Not very far from one million of pounds sterling.

9.—*Q.* What amount of money has been spent actually in providing interest and sinking-fund for the bondholders?

A. Close upon two millions sterling.*

10.—*Q.* What amount of mahogany or silver ore has ever been imported into this country in accordance with the prospectuses?†

A. The mahogany and silver ore were actually exported from Honduras at a loss, for the simple reason that the distracted state of the country rendered the bringing of each product to market so much more expensive than formerly, owing to the almost total absence of labour.

11.—*Q.* Is it true that many formidable engineering difficulties will be met with on the second and third sections of the line of railway?

A. I cannot answer this positively from my own experience, because I have not examined the line practically; but every authority who has done so agrees that the remaining portion of the railway can be constructed within a reasonable time, without meeting more than the ordinary engineering difficulties.

12.—*Q.* From your great and extended experience of Central America, do you think that, when the railway is finished, it will be as paying a concern as the Panama Railway?

---

* *Note by the Author:* An exaggerated statement.

† A small remittance of silver sent by General Medina's Government, was purchased of miners in Honduras and sent to Europe to represent the produce of mines worked by the Government, with money remitted from Europe for that purpose.

A. So far as I am concerned, I am decidedly of opinion that the Honduras Inter-oceanic Railway will prove a much better permanent investment than the Panama Railway itself; and I am strongly confirmed in this opinion by my friend Mr. George B. Kerferd, Consul of Honduras at Liverpool, whose experience of more than a quarter of a century of the commerce of Spanish America renders his opinion peculiarly trustworthy and valuable.

These questions comprise the pith of the inquiries made of me from time to time; but I repeat that, should any gentleman present wish to ask any further questions, every opportunity will be afforded him. I want, however, to point out that, after an experience of six months of careful inquiries and consideration into the affairs of Honduras, I have convinced myself that no enterprise, such as the Inter-oceanic Railway, has ever met with such a series of unfortunate and absolutely unforeseen drawbacks as this has, and that this is the real, sole, and only cause of the disappointment of those I now see around me—a cause which will be removed by the continuance of peace in Honduras, on which the commissioner direct from Honduras will shortly give you his views. I think I also ought to draw your attention to this fact, that the operations in Europe of financing the various loans have been rendered more than usually difficult and expensive by the occurrence of no less than two wars almost within that period, to say nothing of the financial panic of 1866, all of which made it peculiarly difficult to raise the necessary funds; and then, when the funds with great difficulty were obtained, the greater portion has been swallowed up in paying interest and drawings, instead of being devoted to the railway, simply because the internal discord of the Republic put a summary stop to public works.

And now, gentlemen, the painful task devolves upon me of detailing to you, in the most succinct manner, the events which have occurred since my meeting you in this same room in the summer of last year. I will not enlarge upon the strenuous exertions which I have made to arrange financially for meeting the obligations of Honduras and completing the Inter-oceanic Railway.

I do not take any credit, but I feel proud to state to you that I have been over to the Continent no less than ten times on your business; and that, after great trouble and anxiety, it was finally arranged to issue a loan in France, from the proceeds of which the coupon and drawing might be paid, and the works of the Inter-oceanic Railway be vigorously prosecuted. The arrangements, under the best auspices which could be obtained in Paris, were completed, the necessary formalities with the French Government were concluded, and the loan brought out in Paris and the provinces at very great expense, and, as was afterwards proved, with a success which exceeded the most sanguine anticipations. But the well-founded hopes which I ventured to express to you in my circular of the 12th of December last, were not destined to be realized. Monsieur Victor Herran, Minister Plenipotentiary of Honduras in Paris, and his son-in-law, Monsieur Eugène Pelletier, Consul-General of Honduras in Paris, from motives the baseness of which I will not condescend to enlarge upon, having failed to extort from me, through the Honduras bankers in Paris, the sum of £40,000 and £16,000 respectively, laid an information before the French authorities that I had falsely assumed the title of Special Commissioner, and intended to swindle the French public out of the proceeds of the loan.

These assertions, however transparently ridiculous, had upon me a most serious effect. I was summarily arrested at my hotel without the slightest intimation upon what grounds, lodged in the cells like a common felon, dragged before the judge *twice* with a chain round my wrist, and incarcerated for forty-six hours under circumstances which I disdain to excite your feelings by narrating. I will not enlarge upon what I had to endure; but, fortunately, documents seized by the police testified to the baseness, the cowardice, and the deliberate falsehood of Messrs. Herran and Pelletier. Gentlemen, it is my duty to tell you that two more unworthy men it has never been my misfortune to meet with. You will hardly believe that when the Commissioner of Honduras (Dr. Bernhard) called upon Monsieur Victor Herran, on the 27th of December last, and asked him where Captain Bedford Pim could be found, that he replied, Captain Bedford Pim was in London, although he well knew that at that very moment Captain Bedford Pim was incarcerated in the common cell of a French prison, at his own instance. Not only that, but as a proof that Messrs. Herran and Pelletier were both thoroughly cognizant of every step taken by Don Carlos Gutierrez, the Honduras Minister Plenipotentiary in London, the former, M. Herran, sent his son-in-law, M. Pelletier, to Brussels to Don Carlos, who was at that time delivering his credentials from Guatemala to the King of the Belgians, when M. Pelletier, in the name of M. Herran, declared his entire approval of the steps taken, and, after making himself master of the terms of the contract, stated, in the presence of three witnesses, whose letters are appended, that both himself and his father-in-law would give every possible support to the loan.

Before leaving the painful subject of the disgraceful conduct of these two men, I will quote the following extract from the declaration of M. Seegmann, financial agent of Honduras, on this subject.

This gentleman was arrested at the same time as myself, and, being a Bavarian, was possibly in a more dangerous position than I was, for Paris being still in a state of siege, legal security for person or property can scarcely yet be relied upon.

After narrating the particulars of two or three visits paid to him (Mr. Seegmann) at the Financial Agency of Honduras since the 16th of December, he goes on to say :—

"I learned nothing (from M. Pelletier) during the next day, Monday, 23rd ; only about half-past five p.m. M. Nouette Delorme gave me notice that he had been informed by M. François, editor of the *Droit* newspaper, that a protest was to be inserted in his paper the next morning. In spite of my great repugnance, I thought it my duty to go to M. Pelletier, at his hotel at Passy, to demand explanations from him. M. Pelletier was not in, but Madame Pelletier in his absence thought she could assure me that her husband was a complete stranger to the fact I mentioned. However, I waited nearly three quarters of an hour for M. Pelletier, and just as I was going away, as seven o'clock struck, M. Pelletier came in and confirmed what his wife had said. Returning home at once, I found M. Nouette Delorme there again, who told me that he had been informed, and that in effect M. François had received for his paper a protestation, of which he did not think it his duty to point out the authorship, but that at the same time he had been told to await ulterior orders before inserting it. I immediately returned to M. Pelletier, to correct the too great positiveness of my former assertion. M. Pelletier received me most graciously, and repeated to me that he had nothing to do with what might have been done in the *Droit* newspaper; that he had no intention of acting in any way at the present moment, and that he would do nothing without giving me notice. *The next morning, Dec. 24th, his protest appeared in the 'Droit.'* ...

"M. Pelletier, whilst the notary was at work on the 26th of December, tried to enter into conversation with me. I let him talk. He said to me among other things:

"1st. This can do you no harm. We look on you as an intelligent, faithful treasurer-paymaster, and we are especially anxious that your work in the payment of the coupons should not be interrupted for a moment.

"2nd. It is lucky for you that the issue cannot take place just now. The Honduras Government would have suffered a disgraceful check, but we will take it up again in six months with every chance of certain success."

A certified copy of the lengthy document from which the above extracts have been taken has been laid before the Juge d'Instruction, M. Matthieu de Vienne.

I have now only to remark, on the personal part of the subject, that every effort will be made to bring Messrs. Herran and Pelletier to justice. My case will be formally laid before the English Government; the French Government will be officially informed of the conduct of those persons who thus prostitute their diplomatic position to serve their own ends; and it remains to be seen if M. Thiers will ever again receive either of these men; while Don Carlos Gutierrez, my colleague Mr. Kerferd, as well as myself, have officially laid before the Government of Honduras all the facts, with a view to the immediate dismissal of the two men who have done all in their power to dishonour the country they so unworthily represent. After their dismissal, and when no longer clothed with immunity by their official character, they will have to answer to me for their disgraceful behaviour; and, in view of that event, I have already taken the necessary steps to prevent their escape, by employing detectives never to lose sight of either of them.

The letters of Mr. Kerferd and myself to the Government of Honduras, and that of Don Carlos Gutierrez addressed to me, are herewith appended :—

"4, Westminster Chambers, London, S.W.;
Jan. 1, 1873.

"Excellency,—I have the honour to inform your Excellency, that after devoting my best energies as Special Commissioner of Honduras for the last six months towards procuring the necessary funds to meet the obligations of Honduras, and complete the Inter-oceanic Railway, and after the successful issue of a new loan in Paris, the proceeds of which were calculated to effect the immediate object in view, His Excellency Mons. Victor Herran, Minister Plenipotentiary of Honduras in Paris, assisted by his son-in-law, Mons. Eugène Pelletier, Consul-General of Honduras in Paris, caused such protestations and false informations to be laid before the French Government as to occasion the forcible withdrawal of the new loan, at the same time subjecting me to the treatment of a common felon. The motives for this base act are on a par with the baseness of the act itself, but by the enclosed documents your Excellency will be made aware of the dastardly means by which MM. Herran and Pelletier endeavoured to accomplish their ends.

"Fortunately, being well known, and holding a good position, the ambassador of England was soon able to satisfy the French authorities of my *bona fides*. But I shall not at present trouble your Excellency with any details of the sufferings and indignity to which I have been subjected, but rather most earnestly draw your attention to the disastrous results which have arisen, and must ever arise, to the Government of your Excellency by retaining such unworthy representatives in Paris. In fact, as your respected representative in London, Don Carlos Gutierrez, will inform you, it is absolutely necessary that MM. Herran and Pelletier be at once dismissed in vindication of the honour of Honduras, rather than wait until the Government of the country to which they are accredited—France itself—declines to receive them. I think it is my duty to inform your Excellency, without loss of time, of this occurrence, although I cannot enter fully into the details, as there is not time before the mail starts, but I shall lay the whole subject before your Excellency by the next mail.

"As the Special Commissioner appointed by His Excellency Don Carlos Gutierrez on behalf of the Government to endeavour to restore the credit of Honduras, and relieve the Government of all its embarrassments, I feel bitterly that, at the very moment when success was assured, and without the slightest personal intimation from Messrs. Herran and Pelletier—indeed, I have never spoken to either of those persons in my life—they should have taken a step which must leave grave consequences behind it, and which certainly was not in the interests or for the benefit of the country they unfortunately represent.

" I have the honour to be,

" Your Excellency's obedient Servant,

(Signed) " BEDFORD C. T. PIM,

" To His Excellency, " Captain R.N., and Special Commissioner."
The President of Honduras, Comayagua."

" London, *Jan.* 6, 1873.

" Dear Sir,—The Supreme Government of the Republic of Honduras will learn with pain and astonishment the cruel hardships to which you have been subjected in Paris, in consequence of the acts of the Consul-General of that Republic in France.

" As you are well aware, for some time past I have endeavoured to secure the co-operation and to act conjointly in all Honduras matters with my colleague, Señor Don Victor Herran, Minister of the Republic in Paris. To this end, as you know, in the loan contract concluded with you and Mr. George B. Kerferd, the 3rd of December last, I stipulated that the said contract should also be approved and signed by Mr. Herran, and requested you to see him immediately on the subject.

" To secure Mr. Herran's co-operation, I wrote to him, on the 1st and 3rd of December last, the private letters of which I enclose herewith correct translations.

" Mr. Herran did not think proper to answer my letters in writing, but on the 5th of December, M. Eugène Pelletier, his son-in-law, and Consul-General of Honduras in Paris, called upon me at the Hôtel Belle Vue, Brussels, where I was staying. There, and in the presence of the Rev. James Conolly (Clerk), of the Catholic Church of 'Our Lady,' Kentish Town ; of Mr. Frank A. Mori ; and Mr. Charles F. Denny, he (M. Pelletier) informed me on the part of Mr. Herran that he (Mr. Herran) had received instructions from the Honduras Government to confine himself to diplomatic affairs, and not to mix himself in financial matters, and that in consequence of the said instructions he could neither approve nor disapprove officially the above-mentioned contract. M. Pelletier, however, added on the part of Mr. Herran that he was willing to do his utmost in his extra-official capacity, both in Europe and in Honduras, to aid the success of these negotiations for the finishing of the Inter-oceanic Railway, and fulfilling the Government's financial obligations.

" M. Pelletier further added that Mr. Herran considered the steps we were about to take for the issue of the projected loan as the wisest course we could adopt in the present circumstances.

" In answer to M. Pelletier, I said, ' In view of your declarations, and of the support and aid offered by Mr. Herran, I will consent to sign the projected contract loan,' and accordingly, and in his presence, affixed my signature to it.

" With reference to your appointment as commissioner for the financial matters in Europe, you can inform the French authorities that I have conferred upon you that appointment ; in the exercise of the full powers conferred upon me by the Honduras Government, of which you have a perfect knowledge. As you are well aware, those powers were previously examined by Mr. Sharp, by Mr. Wynne, both eminent solicitors of London, by Mr. Grisar, by Messrs. Dreyfus-Scheyer, by their own solicitors, by Mr. George B. Kerferd, and by several other eminent lawyers and business men, and they all unanimously declared that the said powers were in every respect *perfect, valid*, and *ample*. Regarding this point it is impossible to raise the *slightest doubt*.

"I am persuaded that when you present these documents to the enlightened French authorities, in whose justice and impartiality I repose the most *absolute confidence*, they will at once exonerate you from all blame and censure.*

"With the assurances of my highest consideration, believe me, my dear Sir,
"Yours truly,
"CARLOS GUTIERREZ,
Minister Plenipotentiary of Honduras.
"Captain Bedford Pim,
Special Commissioner of the Honduras Government, &c."

"*Jan.* 1, 1873.

"Most Excellent Sir,—I take the liberty of addressing this communication to your Excellency, with the view of bringing to the knowledge of your supreme Government the unfortunate events which have occurred during the last few days in connexion with the new loan, designed for the purpose of completing the Inter-oceanic Railway and paying the dividends on the English and French loans.

"Doubtless the illustrious representative of the Supreme Government, Don Carlos Gutierrez, has already, in pursuance of his duty, informed your Excellency of all that has happened in this matter.

"If not, I venture to ask your Excellency's permission to explain and lay before you so much as has come under my cognizance, and the part which I have taken in this affair. For this purpose I must enter into some explanations, and refer to what has passed during several months up to the present time.

"After the unfortunate result of the attempts made in London to raise a loan for the formation of a Ship Railway and the completion of the Inter-oceanic Line in course of construction, the bondholders in this country began to get uneasy, and to manifest their apprehension that the Supreme Government of Honduras would be unable to make good its promises, or to carry out its intentions successfully to an end; and a thousand doubts were expressed of the probable ability of the said Supreme Government to face its engagements, or to pay the dividends which would fall due at the end of the year.

"In order to reassure these bondholders, it was deemed indispensable that a general meeting of Honduras bondholders should be convened, and such explanations as appeared advisable offered to them, as the only means of preserving the credit and reputation of the Honduras Government.

"To carry this into effect, a man of mark and high social position was required —one whose reputation was sufficiently recognized to enable him to preside at the meeting.

"It was extremely difficult to find a person who at the same time possessed

---

* In fact, Captain Pim, after having been set free, was exonerated from blame, the French tribunals having dismissed the case.

the requisite ability and fulfilled the other indispensable conditions, and who would undertake so thankless and onerous an office. His Excellency Don Carlos Gutierrez was so fortunate as to secure for the performance of this duty Captain Bedford Pim, a distinguished officer of the British Royal Navy, a man of high social position, and well known in the City.

"With the above specified object, His Excellency Don Carlos Gutierrez conferred on this gentleman the appointment of 'Special Commissioner of Honduras.'

"Captain Bedford Pim issued to all the bondholders a circular informing them of the meeting about to take place. This meeting was actually held, and, thanks to the ability and tact of the Special Commissioner, the result was perfectly satisfactory; for the bondholders supported Captain Bedford Pim's proposals, and unanimously resolved that he merited, and might rely upon, the support of the bondholders.

"Up to this point things had gone as well as could be wished, and most of those interested congratulated His Excellency Don Carlos Gutierrez, as the Supreme Government is doubtless aware.

"Matters were in this position when it began to be considered what would be the best means of obtaining the funds necessary for completing the Inter-oceanic Railway, and continuing the payment in Europe of the dividends which would become due.

"After a full discussion of various schemes, it was resolved to endeavour to raise a loan in Paris of five million pounds sterling (nominal) under certain conditions, which this Government is aware of; and it was then that His Excellency Don Carlos Gutierrez did me the honour of associating me with Captain Bedford Pim, to assist him in the undertaking; giving to us both authority, under the powers which he (the said Minister) had received, to raise the above-named loan on the conditions determined on.

"We remained for some time in Paris, treating with the principal bankers of that city, to induce them to undertake the new loan. But, in spite of our endeavours, we could not attain success, as these bankers pretended that the credit of Honduras was not sufficient to enable another loan to be placed; so that we were under the sad necessity of abandoning that idea.

"Nevertheless, as the time was approaching for the payment of the coupon of the English bonds, due on the 1st of January. 1873, and to save as far as possible the credit of the Government, we resolved to make a final attempt; because it was evident that, should the coupon and drawing not be paid in January, the credit and reputation of the Honduras Government would be ruined for ever.

"It was thereupon decided that, without paying any more attention to the opinions of the Paris bankers, the loan should be issued under the management of the 'Financial Agency of Honduras,' which had existed in Paris since the issue of the first loan, for the purpose of paying the dividends, &c.

"The preliminaries were arranged, and, persuaded that our efforts this time would achieve a brilliant success, we applied to His Excellency Don Carlos Gutierrez to obtain the necessary powers. This gentleman was then in Brussels, engaged on a diplomatic mission, and, on being informed of the new scheme, he did us the honour of entirely approving of it; but, out of deference to his colleague in Paris, declined to give us the indispensable powers till he should have consulted His Excellency Don Victor Herran, Minister of Honduras at Paris.

"This latter gentleman was requested to make himself conversant with all the documents, and to give, along with Sr Gutierrez, a joint approval and authorization. Nevertheless, although he approved the scheme, he informed Señor Don Carlos Gutierrez that he was unable to give his official authorization for want of the requisite powers, and the said Don Victor Herran added that he had received most distinct instructions which would prevent his taking any part in matters of finance, and that he devoted himself exclusively to his diplomatic duties.

"However, he sent his son-in-law, Monsieur E. Pelletier, the Consul-General of Honduras, to Brussels to see Don Carlos Gutierrez; and accordingly M. Pelletier travelled thither in company with two friends of Captain Bedford Pim, and saw H. E. Señor Minister Gutierrez; and explained to him that though Señor Herran could not take any active part in the issue of the loan, still, in so far as he the said M. Pelletier could, he would be at his disposal to promote the success of the undertaking; being convinced that it was not only the best, but the only means of saving the credit of the Government of Honduras, already so much compromised.

"Under these circumstances His Excellency Don Carlos Gutierrez gave full powers that the loan should be effected by the said 'Financial Agency of Honduras,' under the auspices of Messrs. Dreyfus, Scheyer, and Co., who undertook to prepare and carry out everything connected with the operation.

"Preparations were pushed forward, and Captain Bedford Pim and myself expended a very considerable sum on the preliminary arrangements, public announcements, and newspapers.

"On the 23rd of December last all the Paris papers, and most of those in the provinces, announced that the subscription was opened; and the contributions received on the first day exceeded our most sanguine hopes.

"The loan was covered, and gave a most brilliant result.

"Nevertheless, on the 24th of December, Señors Herran and Pelletier published in the Paris newspapers a 'public protest,' wherein they declared that the loan was a fraud, that Captain Pim was an adventurer, and was acting without authorization.

"Great was our surprise when this announcement appeared, as such an event could not have been anticipated after all that had occurred. Naturally, after this announcement, we had no option but to abandon the operation; the loan was withdrawn, and the money already in the chests of the Honduras agency was refunded to the public.

"Unfortunately this scandalous incident did not terminate here; for the said Señors Herran and Pelletier had the audacity to institute criminal proceedings against Señor Bedford Pim, and to cause him to be arrested, and (Paris being still under the law of a state of siege) to be manacled and dragged through the principal streets of Paris to the Prison, wherein he was treated like a criminal, remaining in that condition for two whole days; and he was only set at liberty on depositing a sufficient sum to guarantee his appearance before the proper authority when called upon.

"This abuse, as arbitrary as prejudicial to everything, has excited the minds of all who are in any way interested in the welfare of Honduras, and is, I believe, sufficient to ruin for ever in Europe its credit and reputation, unless the Supreme Government hastens to show publicly its disapproval of the conduct of its representatives in Paris, and dismisses them immediately.

"This, I fear, will be the only way to re-establish, in a great measure, if not wholly, the good name which the Supreme Government of Honduras has, up to this time, enjoyed.

"I much fear, however, that this same affair will cause some complication between the Governments of France and of England, for Captain Pim is not only a gentleman highly respected, and of distinguished family, but is also a magistrate, and a person well known to the members of this Government.

"It appears to me needless to dilate on the fatal consequences to which this lamentable occurrence may lead, or to tell your Excellency how deeply I have deplored its having taken place, as your Excellency knows perfectly well the interest which I have ever taken in all concerning the welfare of the Republic, and which is abundantly proved by the very fact of my having taken part in the present operation, and supplied the funds required for launching it.

"It now remains to be seen how the difficulty with the English bondholders can be arranged, as the dividends falling due this very day cannot be paid to them.

"The difficulty remains undecided, and Captain Bedford Pim, by request of His Excellency Señor Gutierrez, has consented to preside at the general meeting of bondholders, to take place in London on Monday next, the 6th instant.

"I request your Excellency, if considered advisable, to bring the above to the notice of His Excellency the President of the Republic, excusing my having dwelt at such length on this most important subject, because I considered it my duty to impart to the Supreme Government all that has come to my knowledge.

"I beg your Excellency to receive the renewed assurances of my highest consideration, wherewith

"I am,

"Your Excellency's obedient faithful Servant,

"(Signed)   "GEO. B. KERFERD."

"To His Excellency the Minister of Foreign Affairs
 of the Supreme Government of Honduras."

Gentlemen, I have one or two words more to say on the general question. I presume that bondholders have come here to-day, as men of business, to look calmly into their affairs, and adopt the measures they may deem best to secure their interests; for my part I will spare no exertion to assist them. The Commissioner of Honduras, who has just arrived (Dr. Bernhard), has written a short statement, which he wishes to be read to the meeting, because his command of our language is not so perfect as he could wish. With your permission I will read it, and at the proper time you can ask him any questions.

"Gentlemen,—I arrived only a few days ago from Honduras, charged with a special commission from the Government with reference to the Inter-oceanic Railway in Honduras.

"I can only assure you that the new Government of Honduras has the intention to act in the most honest, straightforward, and scrupulous manner with reference to the completion of the Railway from sea to sea, and will spare no exertions to that end in the interest of the bondholders.

"With this view, I have been invested with full power from the Supreme Government of Honduras to act in connexion with His Excellency Don Carlos Gutierrez, the Minister Plenipotentiary for the said Government to the Court of St. James's, and we are urgently instructed to spare no effort or sacrifice until we have carried our rails from sea to sea. Be therefore assured, gentlemen, that the Government is firmly resolved to act in good faith towards you, and to use every means in their power to uphold its good name in this great country. Once our enterprise is finished, and the numerous resources of that magnificent region developed, Honduras will have far more than the necessary resources to satisfy all its engagements. This, gentlemen, is unquestionable, and no man who knows anything about Honduras can have the slightest doubt about it.

"Dr. BERNHARD,
"Special Commissioner of the Government of Honduras."

This statement is certainly encouraging, and I cannot but think that there is a fair hope that your interests will not suffer after all.

The CHAIRMAN (who was most cordially greeted with loud cheers when he made his appearance, and frequently vehemently applauded during the delivery of the most marked portions of his speech) his narrative of the treatment he had received from the official representatives of France creating lively indignation and general cries of "Shame, shame" from all parts of the crowded hall), then said :—I have now only to invite you to consider the expediency, in the existing position of our affairs, of appointing a committee with ample powers to investigate everything, whether affecting our financial position or the progress and prospects of the Railway ; and, subject to your approbation, I would suggest the adoption of the following resolution:—

"That a committee (not exceeding nine), of which Messrs. Pim, Kerferd, and Haslewood shall be invited to be members, shall be and is hereby appointed—

"1. To investigate the position and ascertain the prospects of the Railway and of the finances of Honduras in respect to each of the existing loans.

"2. To recommend to a future meeting of the bondholders two independent railway engineers of position and experience to be sent, if necessary, to Honduras, for the purpose of making a special survey of the unfinished portions of the line; what sum is really necessary for the completion of the undertaking and the purchase of plant, machinery, and rolling stock; and within what period the line might reasonably be expected to be finished and in working order.

"3. To consider what steps should be taken for the purpose of raising the necessary funds for the prosecution of the work, and for securing the rights and interests of the existing bondholders, and placing their affairs on a satisfactory basis."

I may mention that this resolution has the entire concurrence of His Excellency and of Dr. Bernhard, both of whom pledge themselves, on behalf of their Government, to afford the committee every facility in the prosecution of their inquiries. I hardly like to put the resolution from the chair, because I want the report to go out to the world that everything done here to-day has been done by yourselves—that you have been guided by no one, but have exercised your own independent judgment. (Cheers.) I will only say that I believe most sincerely that the proposed committee, if formed, can in a very short time, with the means and appliances, and the documents which will be supplied to them, form a sound and accurate opinion upon the whole subject, and call you together to submit a scheme by which your interest may be protected, the property completed, and a great and useful work remain for the benefit of all parties. I should have personally preferred not to have been named as a member of the committee. I have not now the strength of mind and limb that I had some years ago. The severe physical exertion I have had to make lately has, you may be sure, not improved my health. In China, hard work and wounds did something to impair my health; but I can assure you that, if I am appointed with the other two gentlemen named in the resolution, who are your Trustees, I will be the faithful servant of the committee. Every scrap of paper, every document which can throw any light on the position of your affairs, shall be cheerfully and frankly laid before them. (Cheers.) I hope, however, under the circumstances, that some gentleman in the room will move the resolution.

A BONDHOLDER: Why does not the gentleman who drew it propose it, if he is a large bondholder?

The CHAIRMAN: The gentleman was Mr. Pike—a well-known official of the House of Commons.

A BONDHOLDER: There can be no objection to the motion being proposed from the chair.

Another BONDHOLDER: Is the chairman a bondholder?

The CHAIRMAN: No; I am not.

A BONDHOLDER: I cannot see how we can do better than have the resolution proposed by the chairman. He has stated so clearly the reasons why it should be adopted, that it can come from no better quarter. (Cheers.)

The CHAIRMAN: Well, if that is your feeling, I will move the resolution, in the hope that it will be seconded by some bondholder on the other side of the table.

A BONDHOLDER: Why not fix a time when the committee shall make their report? Say in the second week in March?

The CHAIRMAN: No, that is not necessary; a month at the utmost will do. In fact, I think that, if the committee go to work vigorously with the materials which will be at their command, they will be able to present at least a first report in little more than a week or ten days. (Cheers.)

A BONDHOLDER suggested that the committee should consist entirely of bondholders and of gentlemen who, in that capacity, had a large stake in the concern. They should do nothing that could be made a handle of against them by their enemies, and the larger the stake of the members of the committee in the undertaking the better. (Cheers.)

In deference to a warm and general expression of feeling on the part of the meeting, Captain Pim was about reluctantly to move the resolution, when

The Rev. Mr. FITZGERALD said he would be happy either to propose or second it.

The CHAIRMAN: The gentleman who last rose is Mr. Fitzgerald. At the last meeting he gave me a great deal of trouble, and he has a very large stake in the concern, so that I hope you will hear him. Mr. Fitzgerald, except as a bondholder, is a stranger to me; and if he chooses to propose this, I shall be much obliged to him.

Mr. FITZGERALD: If it is your wish, I shall have much pleasure in seconding this resolution. (Cries of "Propose it.") Then I will propose it. (Cheers.) In doing so, gentlemen, I think I am considering your interest as well as my own, for I am sure that nothing will so tend to give public satisfaction or confidence as the fact that a committee of independent bondholders has been appointed, consisting of gentlemen who hold a large stake in the concern. The first duty of that committee will be to report to you at an early meeting what have been the financial arrangements of the Government with respect to these loans. I understand the members of this committee are to have access to all books and papers, and everything connected with the affair, and that it will then be their duty to inquire into the state of the Railway as regards the second and third issues. I understand the first section is entirely completed, and in good working order. The committee will have to inquire what time it will take to complete the Line, and it will be their duty to recommend to an adjourned meeting what financial arrangements can be made in conjunction with the Minister at St. James's and our friend here, Dr. Bernhard, to raise funds sufficient to complete the Railway and pay the bondholders a certain rate of interest. (Cheers.) One word more: in my humble judgment—and I have had some little to do with business—the sooner the resolution is passed, and the gentlemen appointed, the better it will be for all parties concerned.

Mr. J. WALKER seconded the resolution. The reasons for its adoption had been so clearly stated by the chairman and the mover, and so completely commended themselves to the common sense of all present, that it was quite unnecessary for him to add one word in commendation of the resolution.

The CHAIRMAN: Before putting the resolution to the vote, I shall be happy to hear any one who has any observations to make upon the various questions embraced in this very comprehensive resolution. I can, in all sincerity, assure you that I do not wish for anybody to take anything upon trust. I want you all to go away thoroughly satisfied.

Mr. ROBERTS rose and said he had no objection to the appointment of a committee, but he had some questions to ask. (Cries of " Name, name !" " Are you a bondholder ?" and interruption.)

The CHAIRMAN: Pardon me, Sir; will you give me your name, in order that I may ascertain from the book before me whether you are entitled to speak?

Mr. ROBERTS: I am a bondholder personally, and I represent relations who also have larger stakes in the concern than myself.

The CHAIRMAN looked at the Register; not finding Mr. Roberts's name on the list, he asked him if he really was a bondholder, which he declared he was, amidst such interruption and uproar that made it difficult to gather the purport of his observations. As we understood,

Mr. ROBERTS said: I wish to propose an amendment. (Loud cries of "No, no;" "Order;" "Turn him out," &c.) I have a great objection to any gentlemen being on that committee who are not bondholders, and who, consequently, will not look after our interest. I wish to put this question—Where has the money gone to?

Mr. FITZGERALD: That is a question the committee will answer.

Mr. ROBERTS: You say that this Railway will pay as well as the Panama; but what does the Panama pay? It pays 1 per cent.; and if this railway only pays the same amount, it will not pay at all. (Cries of "Question," "Time," &c.) I know the country well. I am engaged in commerce, and know as well as possible the cargoes of mahogany brought home here did not pay. (Cries of "Question," and interruption.) Why should they have sent the mahogany from another place than that through which our Railway runs? (Renewed cries of "Time," "Sit down," &c.) Gentlemen, I see you are not at all inclined to listen to me to-day; but I will call a meeting myself, and I hope that some of you will attend.

Several BONDHOLDERS: Dr. Bernhard.

Dr. BERNHARD, who on presenting himself in response to the call of the bondholders, was received with cheers, said :—I hope, Gentlemen, you will excuse me if I speak very bad English, for I am a foreigner. I may not now be able to make myself heard, for I am a little affected in the throat. Captain Pim has read a letter which shows that I am sent by the Government to see how the Railway can be built, and how things stand here in Europe. The letter read in my name by the chairman contains the expressions of the views of the Honduras Government, which I represent in conjunction with Mr. Gutierrez, the Minister of Honduras at the Court of St. James's. I left Honduras on the 20th of November. In the previous month of October I saw 20 leagues, or more than 60 miles, of the Railway in working order; and trains running every day; while for the second and third sections of the line a great part of the metals are provided. In the place where I live, Tiger Island, there were more than 34 miles of rails stored with locomotives, and everything to commence working when the unfortunate war with Salvador broke out. The materials are there still, and the Government intends to go on with the works at any cost or sacrifice to Honduras. The Government is not at present in a position to pay you your coupons. After two years of war it has no money, but it has the produce, and when once the Railway is finished and emigration comes to the country, the Government will be in possession of funds. It is a beautiful country, that can be cultivated by white emigrants; and when emigration began they would soon see what Honduras produced. I may mention one article of great value that will be forthcoming, and that is copper. There are absolutely mountains of copper, but no roads to bring it down to the coast. I can only repeat that it is the fixed intention of the Government to do all in its power to protect the bondholders, and at the same time to complete the Railroad. (Cheers.)

Mr. FITZGERALD : Gentlemen, if you will allow me, I will tell you my impression of what Dr. Bernhard has said. (Cries of " Spoke," &c.) One section of the railway is entirely completed. (Renewed cries of " Spoke," &c.)

Mr. GRIFFITHS : As to the importance of this resolution, no two opinions can be entertained. Mr. Fitzgerald has spoken well to the point, and I think we are all agreed a committee should be appointed; but, on the other hand, it is necessary that that committee should have the confidence of the bondholders at large. It seems to me that it would be unwise to limit the number of the committee to nine. Appoint nine, but give them power to add to their number any man of note—any man who will take an interest in and devote himself to the work. Nine is so small a number, that there will be a difficulty on occasions in getting a quorum. I therefore propose that the words be added to the resolution—"that the committee, though consisting of nine, should have power to add to their number."

The CHAIRMAN: Allow me to say that you simply anticipate No. 2 resolution, which is to this effect—"That the committee consist of the following gentlemen, with power to add to their number."

The motion was then put, and carried with three dissentients. The result was received with loud cheers by the meeting.

A BONDHOLDER: Now you have carried your favourite resolution. (Cries of "Shame," "Chair," &c.)

The CHAIRMAN: It is not my favourite resolution. It was not drawn by me. My position is this. I come forward to help the bondholders. I have done so for the last six months, and I have no more to do with the loans that have been issued than with that bottle. You must not, therefore, talk about my favourite resolution. You can speak to the second resolution, if you like.

Mr. GRIFFITHS: It is rather illogical and ungrammatical to say that the committee shall not exceed nine, and then afterwards say that they shall have power to add to their number. However, I agree with and therefore propose—"That such committee do consist of the following gentlemen, with power to add to their number, and to call for the production of all necessary books, accounts, and papers, and such oral or documentary evidence as they may deem necessary for the thorough prosecution of their inquiries; and that they report from time to time the result of their deliberations to such future meetings of bondholders as they may deem it expedient to call together."

Mr. PICKERING: Mr. Chairman and Gentlemen,—I have much pleasure in seconding that; but, at the same time, with regard to the names of the persons who should form that committee, it appears to me that it would be almost impossible to carry that out at a meeting like this. There are cheers or groans at every observation that is made, and therefore it is almost impossible to hear anything that is said. I would therefore suggest that some arrangement should be made whereby the chairman, by putting his office at the disposal of the bondholders, might take the responsibility of appointing the committee himself. (Cries of "No, No.") You cannot appoint a committee here; let the chairman select from any list you like.

Mr. WHITLEY: Mr. Chairman and Gentlemen,—With pleasure I rise to support the resolution. I am a working man and a bondholder, and represent a body of working men in the West Riding of Yorkshire. I have come all the way to take a report back to them, as we have no less than £8000 of the bonds. I have listened to the remarks that have been made, and I have great pleasure in supporting the resolution. (Loud cheers.)

The resolution was then put and carried unanimously.

The CHAIRMAN: I beg to announce the resolution is carried unanimously. (Loud cheers.) I wish to add, that I have heard what Mr. Whitley, from the West Riding, has said with great pleasure, and if he will send the addresses of the working-men bondholders, I shall be happy to forward to each of them a paper containing the report of this meeting.

A BONDHOLDER: We should come to an understanding that no gentlemen except those who hold rather a large stake in the undertaking should be on the committee.

Another BONDHOLDER: Say £10,000.

The CHAIRMAN: It strikes me there is not one of you holds £10,000.

A BONDHOLDER: I represent upwards of £20,000 worth of bonds.

The CHAIRMAN: Gentlemen, it seems to me that there are many men who hold only £100, who have as much brains as those holding £10,000. (Laughter and loud cheers.)

A BONDHOLDER: I propose Mr. William Gill.

Another BONDHOLDER: Who is he?

The BONDHOLDER: He is not only a bondholder of £20,000, but he is a man of plenty of brains, and brains in the right place. (Cheers and laughter.)

Another BONDHOLDER: Before that name is put, I should like to make one or two observations. If you go into the question whether a man has brains and where they are placed, I do not think you will ever come to a satisfactory conclusion. If you do that, it will be a matter of impossibility to come to anything satisfactory. If you go into the question of who has brains and who has bonds, how can you, because they do not go together in the Honduras loan? (Laughter and cheers.) It is impossible to discuss this at a meeting of this description. I have heard with painful interest from Captain Pim a statement of what took place in Paris, and I think that it calls for our sympathy more than anything that I have ever known. I am confident that Captain Pim will use his best endeavours in the interest of the bondholders, and I therefore propose that the names of the committee be selected by the chairman. (Loud cheers, and "No, No.")

The CHAIRMAN: I certainly should not undertake the task.

After a rather prolonged and desultory discussion as to the best mode of proceeding with the nomination of the members of the committee,

The CHAIRMAN said he did not wish in the slightest degree to interfere with the full liberty of the bondholders, but he ventured to suggest that, as the Railway was an international as well as an interoceanic one—as four nationalities were concerned in it, Honduras, France, England, and the United States—it would be well that American interests should be represented on the committee. Two gentlemen of New York, who occupied high positions, and who were also engineers of great eminence, had been suggested—he meant Mr. Sickles, and Major General Course, of the United States Engineers. He hoped the suggestion would be fairly considered. (Cheers.)

The election then proceeded, and the following gentlemen were declared by the chairman to be duly appointed :—Messrs. Fitzgerald, Walter Armstrong, J. Higgins, Sickles, Digby Seymour, and Major General Course.

The BONDHOLDER who nominated Mr. W. Gill said he thought that gentleman had been elected.

The CHAIRMAN said his name had not been put to the meeting, but that it was competent for the committee, acting upon the power granted to them by the resolution, to appoint Mr. Gill, or any other bondholder who might be desirous of serving upon the committee, and who possessed the necessary qualifications. For his own part, he should certainly urge that course.

MR. DIGBY SEYMOUR, Q.C., said he had been called upon to propose a resolution. (Prolonged interruption.) The learned gentleman, on resuming, said he should not detain the meeting long, and he did not doubt but that the bondholder at the end of the room would have ample opportunity of speaking to the resolution he had to propose. And he might assure him that, for his part, he would be the first to cheer him and endeavour to obtain for him an audience. And he desired to take this opportunity of expressing the opinion he held, that he did not think that there should be any attempt to silence any one who desired to address the meeting; but at the same time, and speaking rather for those he represented, connexions and friends as well as his own interest, he could not help thinking that it would be eminently desirable for the good of all concerned, if the meeting were to refrain from entering into any lengthened and detailed discussion, which would occupy their time to no benefit, and which was the very province of the committee they had resolved to appoint. Nothing, in his opinion, would prove so injurious to their interests as hastily-put questions involving hasty and inconsiderate replies. Now, passing on from that, however, to the resolution which had been put into his hand for submission to the meeting, he might say that the resolution he had to propose was one which appealed at once and directly to the hearts, and feeling, and right-minded sympathy of every gentleman and lady in this assembly—it was the presentation of the cordial thanks of the meeting to Capt. Bedford Pim. (Loud and prolonged cheering.) He asked the permission of the meeting to refer briefly to a somewhat personal matter. On entering the room that day, he had not had the slightest intention or idea that his name would be proposed as a member of the committee; but when Mr. Fitzgerald thought it his duty to select his name as one of the gentlemen to be appointed to act on behalf of the general body of bondholders, and had made it an appeal to him as a matter of duty to accept such a position, then he hoped that he should be the last man to shrink from any responsibility so conferred. (Hear, hear.) And having accepted the position imposed upon him by the unanimous voice of the meeting, of a member of that committee, he would pledge them his word that as much time as he could devote, and all the care and attention he could command, should be given to answering and satisfying all the questions which had been put, and which occupied the minds of the bondholders as to the financial position of the Government, and the condition and progress of the railway itself. (Cheers.) Now, the cordial vote of thanks which he was about to propose should be presented to their gallant chairman, Captain Bedford Pim, had for its object the tendering of their respectful appreciation of his long and tried services in the interests of the Honduras bondholders—(cheers)—and for expressing their deep condolence and sincere sympathy with him in the late unmerited persecutions he had experienced while engaged in the promotion of their interests. (Prolonged cheers.) Naturally, he (the speaker) had his own views, as a lawyer, on the monstrous pretence under the name—the sacred name—of law, but which was, in fact, the violation of all law, whether domestic or international, which had been suffered in the person of Captain Pim. But it was not even a question of the view which a lawyer might take of the matter. He rather spoke in the common sentiments of their common humanity when he distinctly affirmed that in the indignities their chairman had undergone the very first rights of citizenship had been grossly invaded. (Hear, hear.) He did not know what government ruled over Paris at the present moment, nor did he care whether Paris was regarded as being still in a state of siege; but this he knew, that if the cold, inanimate clay which then laid breathless at Chislehurst, and which had so long and ably ruled the destinies of France, once again held the reins of power, he firmly believed that such a wrong would not pass unavenged and unenquired into. (Loud applause.)

He could only hope, in the absence of any action being taken abroad, that the attention of Lord Granville would be called to the indiguity and outrage done to Captain Pim, upon an *ex-parte* statement put forward by interested persons, and when, without an opportunity being afforded their worthy chairman of communicating with his friends so as to obtain his release, he had been sent for two nights into the cold miseries of a Paris dungeon, and had been twice brought before the city magistrates manacled like a common felon. (Loud cries of " Shame.") The resolution he held in his hand expressed better than he could, and in more solemn language, that which he believed went direct to the opinions and sympathy of every right-minded person in the room. (Hear, hear.) It was as follows—" That the cordial thanks of the meeting be and hereby are tendered to Captain Bedford Pim for his able and courteous conduct in the chair, for his persistent efforts in the bondholders' behalf, and for the full and candid explanation given by him of the recent events in Paris (especially of the unjustifiable proceedings by which his efforts were frustrated when on the eve of being crowned with success), together with the expression of deep condolence and sympathy with him under the sufferings and indignities to which he has been subjected, and of strong indignation for those parties whose interference led to such disastrous results, and who wantonly and deliberately sacrificed the interests of the country they represent, and of the bondholders also, to their own personal interests.

A BONDHOLDER seconded the resolution.

Mr. CUFF, amidst much confusion, addressed the meeting. He concluded his remarks, the point of which was lost in the general clamour, by putting the question to Captain Pim whether he were the authorized agent of the Honduras Government?

The CHAIRMAN replied distinctly in the affirmative. (Cheers.)

The resolution was then put, and carried with acclamation.

On the motion of Mr. POLLARD, seconded by the Rev. Mr. FITZGERALD, the following resolution was unanimously passed—" That it be an instruction to the committee just nominated that they should forthwith convey to the Government of Honduras the expression of the conviction of the bondholders that the conduct of Messrs. Herran and Pelletier is such as to call for their immediate dismissal from office, in order to show the bondholders that the Government are resolved to protect their interest to the fullest extent."

The proceedings, which occupied fully two hours, were then brought to a close.

The following letters refer to the evidence that Messrs. Herran and Pelletier were fully conscious in every respect of Captain Pim's appointment as Special Commissioner, and, in fact, of all his proceedings :—

"*Jan.* 9, 1873.

"Dear Sir,—I have been pained and astounded to hear of the indignities recently offered you in Paris, in consequence of your issuing the prospectus of the new loan for the completion of the Honduras Inter-oceanic Railway.

"No one, perhaps, outside the circle of those immediately engaged in the enterprise, knew more about it than myself, owing to the accidental circumstance of my accompanying His Excellency Don Carlos Gutierrez to Brussels, and there becoming acquainted with all the particulars of the projected loan.

"It is but just to you that I should mention a few facts of which I have been an eye-witness and an ear-witness, which will corroborate what Señor Gutierrez had said in his despatch to you, dated Jan. 6, 1873, a copy of which is before me.

"In the first place, I know that Señor Gutierrez not only gave you full powers to issue the loan in question, but repeatedly expressed himself to me perfectly confident that your energy and ability would make it a success. Again, I know that the loan contract of Dec. 3, 1872, was signed by Señor Gutierrez, subject to the approval and counter-signature of Don Victor Herran, the Honduras Minister Plenipotentiary in Paris.

"I can also bear unequivocal testimony to the painstaking, anxious, and I must add, scrupulous efforts made by Señor Gutierrez, not only by means of letters to Don Victor Herran, but in repeated instructions to yourself by word of mouth and by writing, to associate his colleague in Paris in the enterprize; so much so, that Señor Gutierrez gave Don Victor Herran full powers to modify the conditions of the loan contract as his judgment and prudence should direct, binding himself (Señor Gutierrez) to accept and approve of such modifications.

"Moreover, I remember the morning when an interview took place at the Hotel Belle Vue, Brussels, between Señor Gutierrez and M. Pelletier, the son-in-law of Don Victor Herran. M. Pelletier distinctly said in my presence that he was commissioned to declare his father-in-law had no power to take part in issuing the loan. Don Carlos Gutierrez replied that his own powers from the Honduras Government were so ample that he could associate Don Victor Herran in the undertaking; whereupon M. Pelletier distinctly stated his father-in-law's instructions were to confine himself to diplomatic matters, and not to interfere in financial arrangements. I also know that Señor Gutierrez would not sign the contract till he was assured of the non-official approval of his colleague in Paris. I may also say I never, in my experience, witnessed any man, in any matter of business, proceeding with more caution and acting with more straightforwardness and integrity than Señor Gutierrez. No man, I believe, could have discharged more conscientiously the responsible duty that rested on him; and no man, in my judgment, could have been more solicitous to use every honest effort to protect the interests of the Honduras bondholders, and to save the credit and promote the prosperity of his country.

"I am, dear Sir, yours truly,

"Captain Bedford Pim, R.N."   "J. CONNOLLY."

"Redhill, Chislehurst, *Jan.* 8, 1873.

"Dear Sir,—As I understand that M. Eugène Pelletier, in a protest (which has led to serious results in many ways), has asserted that he was not aware of, and did not co-operate in, your efforts to issue a new Honduras Government Loan in Paris, I feel it my duty to state the following facts.

"On the 5th of December last I was informed that an amended contrac with reference to the said new loan had been signed by His Excellency Don Carlos Gutierrez, the Honduras Minister in London, subject to the approval and joint-signature of His Excellency Don Victor Herran, the Honduras Minister in Paris; and I was further informed that M. Victor Herran, although favourable to the means proposed for raising a new loan, declined to sign the contract, on the ground of having had special instructions from his Government (which had not been rescinded) not to interfere in any financial operations, as full power to control and act as was thought best in all Honduras financial matters in Europe was centred solely in His Excellency Don Carlos Gutierrez; and I further understood that he was willing to write His Excellency Don Carlos Gutierrez to this effect, but that under the advice of his son-in-law M. Eugène Pelletier, Consul-General for Honduras in Paris, he thought it best to send the latter gentleman, M. Pelletier, to personally communicate the same to His Excellency Don Carlos Gutierrez. Therefore M. Mori and myself, under your instructions, met M. Pelletier by appointment the same afternoon, and proceeded with him to Brussels—where he (Don Carlos) was temporarily staying—in order to get His Excellency to remove the proviso regarding M. Victor Herran, in reference to the previously signed amended contract; and I distinctly remember M. Mori showing M. Pelletier, during our journey, the said contract, which he read, and seemed, so far as my observation went, to approve of. The following morning M. Mori and myself met M. Pelletier by appointment at the rooms of His Excellency Don Carlos Gutierrez, where, after an interview of about two hours, His Excellency the Minister, in the presence of M. Pelletier, cancelled the proviso concerning M. Herran's joint signature; at the same time observing in English, that he would not have done so had not M. Pelletier assured him that he had the moral co-operation of M. Herran, and that he (M. Pelletier) considered that the signature of the amended contract, in order to enable Captain Bedford Pim to take the necessary steps for the issuing of a new loan, was the best means under the circumstances of saving the credit of Honduras, or words to that effect.

"The above facts I can declare, in any way that may be most useful to you, and it is owing to my imperfect knowledge of French that I am unable to speak more strongly on the matter, which my companion, M. Mori, would doubtless be able to do, as he conversed freely with M. Pelletier in that language; but I can declare that, in every step which was taken by M. Mori and myself in order to the final signature of His Excellency Don Carlos Gutierrez, M. Pelletier appeared to give us his sympathy and cordial co-operation, and certainly by no word or sign expressed to us any disapproval of your declared object—viz., the carrying out our instructions for facilitating the issue of the new loan.

"Yours obediently,
"(Signed)   "C. F. DENNY."

"To Captain Bedford Pim, R.N.,
    4, Westminster Chambers."

The first meeting of the committee was held at the offices of the Central American Association, 4, Westminster Chambers, Victoria Street, London, S.W., on Tuesday, Jan. 14, 1873. Digby Seymour, Esq., Q.C., was elected Chairman, and Mr. Tucker, Secretary.

A draft letter to His Excellency the President of Honduras, enclosing the "Instruction" of the general meeting of bondholders, passed on the 10th instant, was agreed to, and ordered to be forwarded at once.

IX.

THE MINISTER M. HERRAN AND THE CONSUL GENERAL M. PELLETIER'S JOINT ANSWER TO CAPTAIN PIM'S ACCUSATIONS.

THE different charges brought by Captain Bedford Pim, at the meeting on the 10th of January, against the Minister of Honduras at Paris, M. Victor Herran, and against the Consul General M. Eugène Pelletier, were answered by the latter gentlemen in a letter addressed to the London "Daily Telegraph," and their letter was also published in some French newspapers. It is inserted here in the original language, in order to preserve its native force and vigour.

"*A M. le Propriétaire Rédacteur-en-chef du ' Daily Telegraph,'
à Londres.**

"Paris, 16 *Janvier,* 1873.

"Nous lisons, dans votre journal du 11 Janvier, imprimé à Londres, et vendu à Paris, sous la rubrique, ' Honduras Railway Loans,' le compte-rendu d'un meeting tenu par le ' Capitaine Bedford Pim.'

---

* [TRANSLATION.]
"*To the Editor of the Daily Telegraph, London.*
"Paris, 16 *January,* 1873.

"We have read, in your number of January 11th, printed in London and sold at Paris, under the heading ' Honduras Railway Loans,' the report of a meeting held by ' Captain Bedford Pim.'

"Dans ce meeting notre nom est prononcé, et il est fait, à notre sujet, des déclarations tellement inexactes et insensées que nous ne doutons pas un seul instant que votre impartialité ne donne accès à notre lettre de rectification dans votre plus prochain numéro.

"Le Capitaine Bedford Pim dit que M. Victor Herran, ministre plénipotentiaire, et M. Eugène Pelletier, consul général du Honduras, n'ayant pu obtenir de lui, par l'entremise des banquiers du Honduras à Paris, l'un une somme de £40,000, l'autre une de £16,000, se sont opposés à l'émission projetée en France; il ajoute que tout effort sera tenté pour amener M. Herran et M. Pelletier devant la justice, et que, de concert avec ses associés, il a formulé une demande en révocation au Gouvernement du Honduras; que dès que M. Herran et M. Pelletier seront destitués et ne se retrancheront pas derrière des immunités, il exercera ses revendications contre eux; qu'en vue de cet événement il a pris des dispositions pour les empêcher de quitter le territoire français.

"Avant de porter une plainte en diffamation contre les auteurs de ces calomnies, sans savoir si cette mesure aurait son effet à Londres, nous mettons au défi M. Bedford Pim de venir en France répéter ce qu'il a dit; nous lui donnons le démenti le plus formel et le plus catégorique, et nous le sommons de dire, sous peine d'imposture, le nom des Banquiers auxquels il prétend faire allusion, nous réservant une enquête à ce sujet.

"Il n'y a aucun effort à tenter pour amener un coupable devant

"At that meeting our names were mentioned, and such incorrect and absurd statements were made in regard to us, that we cannot for a moment doubt that you will, out of impartiality, insert our rectification in your next number.

"Captain Bedford Pim said that M. Victor Herran, Minister Plenipotentiary, and M. Eugène Pelletier, Consul-General of Honduras, having been unable to obtain from him, through the medium of the Honduras bankers at Paris, the one a sum of £40,000, and the other a sum of £16,000, opposed the projected issue in France; he also said that every effort would be made to bring M. Herran and M. Pelletier to justice, and that, in concert with his companions, he had drawn up an application to the Honduras Government requiring their dismissal; that as soon as M. Herran and M. Pelletier should be dismissed, and could not entrench themselves behind their immunities, he would take his revenge upon them, and that, in expectation of that event, he had taken precautions to prevent them from leaving French territory.

"Before we bring an action for defamation against the propagators of these calumnies, without knowing whether such a measure would be effective in London, we defy Mr. Bedford Pim to come to France and repeat what he has said; we give him the lie most formally and categorically; and we challenge him to tell, on pain of imposture, the name of the bankers to whom he pretends an allusion, reserving to ourselves an inquiry on this subject.

"Nothing can be done to bring a delinquent to justice in France. We la justice française. Nous déclarons que, si le Gouvernement du Honduras n'approuve pas hautement notre conduite, dont le caractère de loyauté est si élevé qu'il étonne M. Bedford Pim et consorts, nous le prions de recevoir notre démission; et libres de toute attache, nous poursuivrons une enquête dont les révélations offriront plus d'une surprise à M. Bedford Pim et consorts. Afin que M. Bedford Pim puisse agir de suite et sans entrave contre nous, M. Victor Herran dépose immédiatement ses immunités diplomatiques; et quant à M. Pelletier, consul-général d'un pays étranger, mais toujours citoyen français d'origine, et ne jouissant d'aucune immunité, il n'a nulle intention d'en invoquer, et nulle envie de quitter le territoire français. Faut-il démontrer ce que chacun touche déjà du doigt, l'inanité de la tentative Bedford Pim ? Aucuns pouvoirs n'étaient énoncés dans les prospectus de l'Emprunt, aucunes des formalités essentielles n'avaient été remplies; sans autorisation du Ministre des Affaires étrangères, comme sans avoir pu faire insérer sa souscription au *Journal Officiel*, doit-il s'étonner M. Bedford Pim d'avoir éveillé les susceptibilités du ministère public, sauvegarde de la société ?

" Qu'il ne s'en prenne donc qu'à lui-même de sa mésaventure, et qu'il s'informe et nous apprenne ce qui adviendrait à Londres à un sujet français agissant dans les conditions analogues.

" Nous devons nous abstenir, en raison de l'instruction qui se poursuit, de juger cette tentative avortée; mais nous tenons à honneur de déclarer, haut et ferme, que l'opinion publique ne saurait être

---

declare that if the Honduras Government does not approve our conduct in every respect, the character of which is so high that it astonishes Mr. Bedford Pim and his confederates, we beg it to accept our resignation; and, freed from every tie, we will prosecute an inquiry of which the revelations will surprise, once and again, Mr. Bedford Pim and his confederates. In order that Mr. Bedford Pim may go on and act without obstruction against us, M. Victor Herran at once relinquishes his diplomatic immunities; and as for M. Pelletier, Consul-General of a foreign country, but still a French citizen by birth, and not enjoying any immunity, he has no intention of claiming it, and no wish to depart from French territory. Is it necessary to show that everyone must be already aware of the absurdity of Bedford Pim's attempt ? No powers were announced in the prospectuses of the loan—none of the essential formalities were observed. Without the authority of the Minister for Foreign Affairs, and without having been able to insert his subscription in the *Official Journal*, could Mr. Bedford Pim be surprised that he had awakened the attention of the public prosecutor, the safeguard of society ?

" Let him blame himself, then, for his mishap, and let him inquire and inform us what would happen in London to a French subject under similar circumstances.

' As an investigation is going on, we will abstain from passing judgment

faussée plus longtemps par les manœuvres de ces hommes, et que le crédit du Honduras en France a été sauvegardé par l'énergie de ses représentants officiels.

"(Signé)   " VICTOR HERRAN.
"EUGENE PELLETIER."

This unfortunate and unexpected affair between MM. Herran and Pelletier and Captain Pim again produced excitement, and led to lamentable contention between those persons, who were bound to proceed in concert and sincerity to promote the undertaking; and again those eternal quarrels went on which had so often occurred amongst the various persons more or less connected with these affairs. Fortunately the diverse nationalities of MM. Herran and Pelletier and Captain Pim, and the difficulty in regard to the competency of the courts before which the question might be brought, postponed the matter *sine die*.

The Committee of Investigation appointed at the meeting of bondholders on the 10th of January, 1873, reported in March of the same year as follows :—

"REPORT OF THE COMMITTEE APPOINTED BY THE HONDURAS BONDHOLDERS AT A PUBLIC MEETING HELD ON THE 10TH JANUARY, 1873.

"The following are copies of the Resolutions which were passed at the meeting :—

"That a Committee (not exceeding nine), of which Messrs. Pim, Kerferd, and Haslewood shall be invited to be members, shall be and is hereby appointed :—

"1. To investigate the position and ascertain the prospects of the Railway and of the Finances of Honduras, in respect to each of the existing Loans.

"2. To recommend to a future Meeting of the Bondholders two independent Railway Engineers of position and experience to be sent (if necessary) to Honduras for

---

on this abortive attempt; but it is our bounden duty to declare, loudly and confidently, that public opinion can no longer be misled by the manœuvres of these men, and that the credit of Honduras in France has been saved by the energy of its official representatives.

(Signed)   "VICTOR HERRAN,
"EUGENE PELLETIER."

the purpose of making a special survey of the unfinished portions of the Line, what sum is really necessary for the completion of the undertaking, and the purchase of plant, machinery, and rolling-stock, and within what period the Line might reasonably be expected to be finished and in working order.

" 3. To consider what steps should be taken for the purpose of raising the necessary funds for the prosecution of the work, and for securing the rights and interests of the existing Bondholders, and placing their affairs upon a satisfactory basis.

" 4. That it be an instruction to the Committee just nominated that they should forthwith convey to the Government of Honduras the expression of the conviction of the Bondholders that the conduct of Messrs. Herran and Pelletier is such as to call for their immediate dismissal from office, in order to show the Bondholders that the Government are resolved to protect their interest to the fullest extent.

" Your Committee held their first meeting on the 14th January, 1873, and continued their meetings twice every week up to the present time, devoting much time and labour to the duties imposed upon them.

" Your Committee in the first instance, acting upon the terms of the foregoing Resolution as to the conduct of Messrs. Herran and Pelletier in reference to Captain Pim, sent out to Honduras a printed Report of the proceedings at the Meeting, and with it a letter calling the attention of the Government to the above Resolution.

" Your Committee commenced their investigation by directing their Honorary Secretary to obtain copies of all contracts and accounts connected with the various loans raised for the Government of Honduras; and, as a preliminary step, letters were written to the Honduras Ministers in London and Paris.*

" The Honduras Minister replied to the letter of the Committee expressing his readiness to afford every assistance and facility in his power to the inquiries of your Committee; and, while reserving for his Government all its rights of non-accountability as a Supreme Power, has willingly placed at their disposal the documents in his possession, but no answer has been received from the Minister in Paris, Monsieur Victor Herran. A member of your Committee went to Paris and saw his Excellency personally, who acknowledged the

---

* See Appendix, No. III.

receipt of the letter from the Committee, but added that he did not intend to reply to it, or account to the Committee or the Bondholders.

"Your Committee proceeded to obtain information from all available sources as to the history and character of the various Loans, and the circumstances under which they were issued to the public; and the result of their enquiries shows that the Loans have been issued under the pressure of financial difficulties and State necessities in a great measure not contemplated at the time of the issue of the said loans.

"Large portions of the money have been expended under the authority of the Government for the purpose, as explained to the Committee, of 'maintaining its credit.'

"Much of the profitless expenditure is attributed to the late unsettled state of Honduras, and the succession of internal wars and revolutions, causing frequent interruptions, and oftentimes total suspension of the works on the Railway; but your Committee have reason to believe there is every prospect of continued peace throughout Central America.

"This state of things has obviously led to exceptionally embarrassing financial operations by the Government in connexion with the loans which, under other circumstances, might have been less onerous.

"Owing to the course pursued by M. Herran, your Committee have not been able to obtain any reliable information with regard to the loan raised in Paris. But with regard to the English Loans of 1867 and 1870, the following summary is submitted:—

In the year 1867 a Loan for £1,000,000 was issued at the net price of £73. 11s. 10¹d.	£735,937 10 0
In the year 1870 a Loan for £2,500,000 was issued at the price of £80 . .	2,000,000 0 0
Total net issue price	£2,735,937 10 0
Out of these Loans there has been paid on the Works of the Railway and for Engineering	562,800 0 0
The Sinking Funds and interest have amounted to	1,246,800 0 0
To and on behalf of the Government and for Mining purposes	165,000 0 0
Carried forward	£1,974,600 0 0

Brought up	£1,974,600	0	0
To expenses on the French Loan account, paid out of these Loans	17,500	0	0
Federal Debt Stock purchased out of these Loans	6,000	0	0
Stock of 1870 Loan, ditto, 168 Bonds at 80 per cent.	13,440	0	0
Cash in the hands of the Trustees	13,000	0	0
	£2,014,540	0	0*
Leaving a balance of about	721,397	10	0
	£2,735,937	10	0

"This sum of £721,000 has been disbursed in various expenses and outlays over a period of six years, including the Commissions on the Loans, and the large amount before referred to as expended by the Government in 'maintaining its credit' during the wars in Honduras and on the Continent.

"The Committee abstain from further comment on the above figures, partly because your Committee are not clothed with sufficient powers to investigate details or distinguish responsibilities, owing chiefly to the fact that the loss and expenditure are mainly the direct acts of the Honduras Government, or have received its express sanction, or that of its accredited representatives, and still more because the Government of Honduras is prepared to make concessions of great magnitude and value to compensate for the losses of the Bondholders, and secure the ultimate completion of the Inter-oceanic Railroad.

"Your Committee conceive it to be in the interest of the Bondholders not to provoke any inexpedient or inopportune discussion with the present executive of Honduras, which has shown every disposition to deal with the Bondholders in a spirit of fairness and cordial co-operation.

"The representatives of the Honduras Government in London have expressed the willingness of that Government to cede in fee simple as security to the Bondholders, and as an annex to the Inter-oceanic Railway, a tract of country equal to 2½ miles on each side of the Railway, from sea to sea, free of all liability to taxes and charges of every description, with power to work, or grant concessions to

---

* *Sic* in original Report, but should be £2,024,540.

work, such of the unappropriated silver and copper mines of the entire State of Honduras as the representatives of the Inter-oceanic Railway shall select.

"Your Committee requested the attendance of Dr. Bernhard, Special Commissioner for Honduras, Consul at Honduras for the German Empire, and resident for upwards of 20 years in Central America, to state his views as to the resources of Honduras, and the present condition of the country. He prepared a Report.*

"A further Report from the pen of Mr. G. B. Kerferd, Member of your Committee, and a gentleman of lengthened practical experience in the commerce of Honduras, will be found in the Appendix (No. III.).

"Since the Public Meeting, three important and encouraging letters, dated the 2nd and 3rd days of December, have been received from Mr. W. A. Brooks, for many years Chief Engineer to the Commissioners of the river Tyne, and the Engineer sent out by Captain Pim to Honduras to report on the position and prospects of the Railway, a gentleman in whose ability and good faith the Committee have grounds for placing implicit confidence.†

"The Commissioners of Honduras in London have cordially co-operated with your Committee in affording every information in their power, and have furnished the funds necessary to send to Honduras two American Engineers of your Committee's nomination, who are now on their way to investigate, examine, and report upon the present state of the fifty-six miles of the Railway which have been completed, the progress made with the remaining portion, the ultimate cost of completion, and the prospects of the whole·undertaking.

"Several schemes for raising further Capital have been submitted to the consideration of your Committee for completing the Interoceanic Line of Railway. Whatever scheme may be ultimately adopted, your Committee are unanimous in recommending that the financial department, now under the control of the Honduras Government, should be transferred to European administration. Your Committee are assured of the willingness of the Honduras Government to transfer all their interest in the Railway to a Limited Joint Stock Company, to be incorporated for the purpose of raising the necessary Capital for the completion of the Railway, the purchase of rolling stock, &c., or to acquiesce in any arrangement by which the interest of the Bondholders through the completion of the Railway can be secured.

"From inquiries instituted by your Committee, they feel no hesi-

---

* See Appendix, No. III. † See Appendix, No. III.

tation in saying that an arrangement can be effected with responsible Contractors, on satisfactory terms for the early completion of the entire Line.

"Your Committee calculate, so far as they have estimates to guide them, that, to provide the necessary funds for such a purpose, it may be necessary to raise a Capital up to £2,000,000.

"Your Committee, in considering the foregoing scheme, have not overlooked the interests or position of the present Bondholders; and, in the event of the Company being formed, they recommend that the Bondholders should have the option of exchanging their Bonds at a price and under conditions to be hereafter determined for Preferential Debentures of the proposed Company, or some such arrangement as shall equitably adjust the security between the new Capital to be provided and that already raised.

"(Printed by Order of the Committee)

"JOHN TUCKER,

"*March*, 1873. *Hon. Sec.*"

"Offices—4, Westminster Chambers,
Victoria Street, Westminster."

The first part of this Report is unfortunately as absurd as it is incorrect, and one can hardly understand how the men of business who formed the Committee could draw up an account from the materials before them in the manner they have done.

They charge the loan of 1867 and that of 1870 at the prices of issue to the public, that is, the first at £73. 11s. $10\frac{1}{2}d.$, and the second at £80. This might have been done if the loans had been wholly subscribed for at the time they were issued. If that had been the case, the account would be clear and decisive, and there would have been no necessity for the expedient of showing a deficit of £721,397 for unknown expenses, and for "maintaining the credit" of Honduras. How much more simple would it have been for the Committee to state the average price at which the loans were placed, for it is notorious that at the beginning of 1872, about half the bonds of those loans were still for sale, and it was necessary to place very many of them at less than 40 per cent. of their value.

The Committee has made another and a greater mistake in the above Report. It is that of not separating the sums produced by the tardy sales of the debentures of the French loan, deposited with Messrs. Bischoffsheim and Goldschmidt and with the Trustees. These had not been subscribed for in Paris at the time of the issue, and they amounted to about a third part of that loan; they were brought to London when the war broke out between Germany and France, for they could not be sold in Paris. From this Report it appears that the London loans, even omitting the deficit of £721,397, put down by the Committee to balance the account, produced an average of 57½ per cent., when in reality, as already stated, they did not produce more than 45 per cent.

Some of the figures on the credit side are also incorrect, especially the amount of £1,236,800 for redemption and interest of the said two loans. And, in consequence of this erroneous Report, unjust suspicion of malversation has fallen upon the persons who have had the direction of these affairs, and on the Government which was endeavouring to "maintain its credit," and thereby diverted enormous sums; when what the Government and its agents endeavoured to do, was to sell the bonds at the only price at which they could place them on 'Change, and apply the proceeds to so many urgent engagements.

The remainder of the Report is devoted to the purpose of showing the bondholders that the Government was disposed to make very important concessions, in order to establish a Company to finish the Railway, and with that object was studying various projects presented to the Committee. It was announced that £2,000,000 were required to complete the Railway, and that it would be necessary to ask the public for them; it was also stated that the Government had very important documents in its possession, recommending the Line and the great resources of the forests and mines of the Republic of Honduras, forwarded by Mr. W. A. Brooks, the engineer sent to Honduras by Captain Pim, by Mr. G. B. Kerferd, a member of the Committee, and by Dr. C. E. Bernhard, the Government Commissioner.

The Committee of Investigation went on with its labours in concurrence with Dr. C. E. Bernhard, and the Trustees, in order to form a Company for the completion of the Railway, and discussed the conditions for its constitution, as well as the concessions it was necessary to require from the Government. Finally, the contracts were made, and they were sent to Honduras to be approved by the Government of the President Don Céleo Arias, if they were considered satisfactory.

X.

MEETING OF BONDHOLDERS ON THE 24TH AUGUST, 1873. —FORMATION OF THE COMPANY TO CONSTRUCT THE RAILWAY.

ANOTHER meeting of bondholders was held at the London Tavern, on the 24th of August, 1873, for the purpose of receiving from the Committee appointed on the 10th of January its final Report upon the investigation of the facts and the means adopted to proceed with the construction of the Line. Mr. Digby Seymour was in the chair.

The Chairman, in a long and eloquent speech, stated the object of the meeting, which was to submit the proceedings of the Committee to the consideration of the bondholders, and to await their judgment on them.

He stated that the three Trustees, Captain Bedford Pim, Mr. Haslewood, and Mr. Kerferd, had retired from the Committee, because they, having been invited at first to join the Committee, rather represented the special interests of the

Honduras Government. Colonel Peel, Mr. A. Clark, and Dr. Evan Desmond had been appointed to fill these three vacancies.

The Chairman afterwards proceeded to give the results of his investigations in regard to the loans; his figures were hardly at all compatible with those given in the Report presented in March, and much less so with the real amounts. He said that no particulars respecting the French loan could be obtained for the last Report, but that some had since been received. He said that there were then in circulation 29,638 Bonds of £100 each, representing a nominal value of £2,963,800; there were also in circulation 8,970 Shares of £20, amounting to £179,400; 177,135 Bonds of £12, representing £2,125,620; and lastly, 789 Shares of £100, representing £78,900 (belonging to the Federal debt). This gives a grand total of £5,347,720.

Neither is this second Report correct. The nominal total of the three loans issued, without including the Federal debt, amounts to £5,990,108; and if, at the date when the Chairman reported, there had only been in circulation (exclusive of the cancelled bonds) the total amount which he stated, then there would have been at the same date the balance of £721,288 in possession of the Trustees (always deducting the Federal debt) cancelled or for sale.

The Chairman then gave an account of the concessions obtained from the Government, for the purpose of serving as a basis for the formation of a Company to complete the Railway; first, the concession of the whole line of the said Railway from Port Cortez in the Atlantic to the Bay of Fonseca in the Pacific, including the 56 miles already constructed; second, five miles of land on each side of the line, from beginning to end; third, the concession of the mines in Honduras belonging to the Government.

He afterwards indicated the principal bases for the formation of the Company to complete the Railway, and the great hopes entertained on account of the concessions obtained and on which the Company was founded. In consequence the meeting passed a resolution approving and confirming all that the Committee had done, and engaging the bondholders to use every kind of exertion to promote the success of the said Company.

Here is the " Memorandum of Association of the Honduras Inter-oceanic Railway Company," as it appears in the Prospectuses circulated :—

"MEMORANDUM OF ASSOCIATION OF THE HONDURAS INTER-OCEANIC RAILWAY COMPANY (LIMITED).

" 1. The name of the Company is the Honduras Inter-Oceanic Railway Company, Limited.

" 2. The Registered Offices of the Company will be in England.

" 3. The objects for which the Company is established are the ollowing :—

(A) To obtain from the Government of the Republic of Honduras and accept concessions or grants of all or any of the following Railways, works, lands, rights, powers, and privileges, viz. :

(a) Such portion of the Honduras Inter-Oceanic Railway as is already completed and open for traffic, or is in course of construction, together with all the stations, houses, buildings, wharves, quays, jetties, and appurtenances thereto belonging or attached, or forming part thereof, together with all the rolling stock, plant, machinery, rails, materials, stores, equipments, and other effects belonging to the Government, and used, or intended to be used, for the construction, equipment, maintenance, or working of the said Railway with its appurtenances, or for any of the purposes thereof.

(b) The land required for the completion of the said Railway from the Atlantic Ocean to the Pacific Ocean, with all necessary and proper wharves, quays, jetties, and other conveniences.

- (c) Such other lands, adjoining or near to the said Railway, as may be agreed on between the said Government and the Company, with such exclusive rights of cutting and exporting timber grown thereon free of duty and other charges, as may also be agreed on.
- (d) Such of the Mines belonging to the Government of Honduras, and at present unallotted, and at the disposal of the State, as may be agreed on between the Government and the Company, subject to such royalty (if any) whether fixed or fluctuating, as may also be agreed upon.

(B) To construct, complete, maintain, equip, and work the said Railway, and to work, let, manage, and grant licenses for the working of all or any of the Company's lands, land rights, timber, mines and mineral rights, and to export sell, and dispose of the produce thereof.

(C) To sell, demise, or otherwise dispose of, all or any of the lands, mines, rights and privileges, or other property of the Company (including the said Railway, with its appurtenances).

(D) To acquire any other concessions, grants, or privileges from the Government of Honduras, or any other foreign Government, and to enter into any contracts with any Government, Corporation, or persons, for any of the purposes of the Company.

(E) To obtain the incorporation of the Company as a Société Anonyme, or Sociedad Anonima, according to the laws of the Republic of Honduras, or any foreign state, relating to joint stock companies.

(F) To do all such other things as are incidental or conducive to any of the foregoing purposes.

" 4. The liability of the members is limited.

" 5. The capital of the Company is £5,347,720, divided into 30,427 Shares of £100 each, to be called A Shares; 177,135 Shares of £12 each, to be called B shares; and 8,970 Shares of £20 each, to be called C Shares.

The shares may be issued as fully paid up to the holders of the bonds of the Honduras Government Railway loans, issued in London in 1867 and 1870, or the loans issued in Paris in the year 1869, or of the Federal debt of the State of Honduras issued in 1867, in exchange for their bonds in the proportion of one £100 share for every bond for £100 in either of the said loans, and so in proportion for bonds of any larger or lesser denomination. The Company may accept from any of the subscribers of this Memorandum bonds of the said Honduras Government loans of 1867, 1869, and 1870, or of the said Federal debt in or towards payment of the shares subscribed for by them respectively at par."

In accordance with this Memorandum of Association, the Prospectus* was published, to convert the bonds of all the Honduras loans into shares of the Company formed to complete the Railway. By means of that conversion the Honduras Government was to be entirely freed from the heavy burden of its loans, the bonds of which were to be converted into shares of the Company, and to be freed also from the general mortgage on all the uncultivated lands and the forests of the State. In exchange, the Government granted to the said Company the whole of the Line already constructed, with all the buildings and materials belonging to it; the necessary lands for the completion of the Line from sea to sea, its stations, piers, docks, and buildings; the right of importing, free from every tax or charge, the materials, engines, and all that should be necessary for, or connected with, the completion of the Line; the right of constructing, fitting up, maintaining, and working the Railway, and of receiving the proceeds of the traffic; all the State lands comprised in a band of territory ten miles wide, or five miles of territory on each side of the Line throughout; a concession for ninety-nine years of all the mines of antimony, copper, iron, silver, and others, including those of coal and marble, belonging to the State, subject to a royalty of 10 per cent. only upon the net profit, after paying a dividend of 10 per cent.

These concessions and conditions were stipulated in two contracts, which bear date the 12th of July, 1873, entered into by the Minister in London and the Special Commissioner,

---

* See Appendix, No. IV.

Dr. C. E. Bernhard, as representatives of the Honduras Government, on the one part, and by the Company on the other part; and in another additional contract, bearing date 1st of December, 1873, entered into by Dr. C. E. Bernhard, as representative of the said Government, and the aforesaid Company. The Governm nt of Honduras, under the Presidency of Señor D. Céleo Arias, ratified those contracts, referring the final approval of them to the Congress which assembled at the close of his Presidential period, and this also ratified them.

But the conversion of the bonds of the Honduras loans into shares of the "Inter-oceanic Railway Company" in no way advanced the Company in regard to the most urgent and direct object, which was to procure the necessary funds for the completion of the Line ; and the "Inter-oceanic Railway Company" was obliged to have recourse to the money market by issuing 20,000 Preference Shares of £100 each at par, as part of the 25,000 Shares of this class, which its regulations gave it power to issue.

Here is the Prospectus of this new combination for the completion of the said Railway :—

"FIRST ISSUE OF 20,000 TEN PER CENT. FIRST MORTGAGE DEBENTURE BONDS OF £100 EACH AT PAR,

" Being part of 25,000 which the Company have power to issue.

"THE HONDURAS INDER-OCEANIC RAILWAY COMPANY LIMITED.

" Debenture Capital £2,500,000.

" *It is proposed to issue this Capital in Bonds of £100 each, bearing interest at 10 per cent. per annum.*

" *The Bonds to be redeemed at par by Annual Drawings, and by the operation of a Sinking Fund, in 25 years.*

" The first Drawing to take place on the 31st of December, 1876, and the drawn Bonds will be paid on the next succeeding 15th day of January, when the interest thereon will cease.

"The Bonds will be issued to bearer, with Coupons, payable half-yearly on the 1st January and 1st July in each year, at the offices of the Company.

"The first payment of interest to take place on the the 1st July, 1874.

"PROSPECTUS.

"These Bonds stand as a first charge by the Railway Company upon all its lands, estates, properties, and revenues, comprising such portion of the Railway as is already in operation, completed or in course of construction, together with the rolling stock, stations, materials, buildings, chattels of every kind, and all rights and privileges conferred by the terms of the Concession held by the Company, including the lands necessary to complete the Line from sea to sea.

"The revenues also, under a Concession for 99 years, from all mines and minerals belonging to the State, subject only to the payment of a small deferred royalty, are included under the same charge.

"In the Concession obtained from the Government are also included almost inexhaustible supplies of hard and other woods, namely, mahogany, rosewood, pine, and other timber of the finest growth and quality; and which, when the means of transit have been completed for conveyance of the same to the ports for exportation to the European markets, one of the largest and most certain sources of profit will be opened up for the bondholders.

"The grants made by the Government of Honduras to the Company have been subsequently confirmed by the existing legislative powers of the State, and take effect immediately.

"It will be seen at once that the varied resources of the Company are abundant, and, when developed, more than sufficient to guarantee prompt payment of interest upon and redemption of the Bonds, as well as to provide for the working expenses of the Line.

"Indeed, when the opening of the Line from sea to sea has been accomplished, experience shows that the revenues will rapidly and progressively increase.

"It may fairly be estimated that the minimum amount to be written off will certainly not be less than after the rate of £80,000 per annum.

"For every £100 debenture the price will be payable as follows:—

On application, deposit	£5
On allotment	5
On 2nd March, 1874	10
On 1st June, 1874	10
On 7th September, 1874	10
On 7th December, 1874	10
On 1st March, 1875	10
On 7th June, 1875	10
On 6th September, 1875	10
On 6th December, 1875	10
On 1st March, 1876	10
	£100

Or the full amount may be paid at any earlier date under discount at 5 per cent.

"Scrip will b issued, which will be exchanged for Mortgage Debenture Bonds on payment of all the instalments.

"In case of no allotment being made, the deposit of the applicant will be returned without deduction.

"The Company reserve to themselves the right to issue the remaining 5,000 Debenture Bonds, which, when issued, will rank *pari passu* with the present issue of 20,000 Debentures.

"Applications in the form annexed to be sent to the Bankers of the Company,* or to C. F. Denny, Esq., Secretary of the Company, 4, Westminster Chambers, Victoria Street, S.W."

"23rd December, 1873."

The subscription for these Preference Shares was received by the public with the same indifference as those for the Honduras loans; and although it was not officially known at the time how much had been subscribed for, because the Company thought proper to keep this secret, it afterwards came out that the said subscription had not exceeded £30,000, an insignificant sum towards enabling the Company to take serious steps for the development of its projects.

Nevertheless, the conversion of the bonds of the Honduras Loans into shares of the Company, began to be effected with

---

* Messrs. Glyn, Mills, Currie, & Co., Lombard Street.

tolerable success, so far that in London and Paris very nearly a third part of the bonds representing the loans had been converted; from which circumstance it may be readily presumed that, if the issue of the Preference Shares had had such success as to assure the intentions of the Company already formed, all or nearly all the bonds would have been eventually converted.

At the very time when the Inter-oceanic Railway Company was endeavouring in Europe to convert the bonds of the Honduras loans into railway shares, and was issuing preference shares to obtain capital in order to complete the work, there was a revolution in Honduras to upset the Government of the President, Señor D. Céleo Arias.

That revolution succeeded, and His Excellency Señor D. Ponciano Leiva was raised to the Provisional Presidency of the Republic by the national will in consequence. He immediately issued the following manifesto :—

" Ponciano Leiva,
"Provisional President by the National Will,
" To the People of the Republic.

" Hondureans: The war which it was indispensably necessary to undertake against the Dictatorship of Señor Licentiate Don Céleo Arias has terminated fortunately. I congratulate you, and rejoice with you on this auspicious event.

" The Hondurean nation, like a traveller escaped from shipwreck, rescued from the anarchy into which it seemed about to be plunged, has entered upon the enjoyment of peace and order—inestimable advantages which the Government intends to secure, by means of the good sense of the nation, and the co-operation of the most enlightened members of society, who are responsible for the irregularities of the rest.

"In accordance with my promises in the manifesto of November 23, after discussion with the Council of Ministers, it has been resolved as follows :

" 1. A decree of amnesty shall be issued for all Hondureans, who are out of the territory of the Republic for political reasons.

" 2. The Judicial Power shall be provisionally reorganized; and

" 3. A National Convention shall be convoked to proceed to the political reorganization of the country, in the form which it may deem most expedient.

"Meanwhile, Hondureans, your safeguards and rights not secured by law shall be respected by the Government, which will in every case be guided by considerations of justice and public convenience.

"Fellow citizens: it is not for me to boast that I am about to implant liberal principles in Honduras, for they have been proclaimed and adopted by our predecessors, ever since the year 21; my feeble efforts will only be directed to perfect them in practice. This is *my* purpose; and, as far as regards yourselves, you are in possession of all your rights: make that legitimate use of them to which you are entitled, without forgetting at the same time your duties towards the State.

"Ponciano Leiva."

"Comayagua, 24*th* January, 1874."

This change of Government gave rise to doubts and discussions as to the legality of the Congress assembled during the Presidency of Señor D. Céleo Arias, and as to whether the ratification of the concessions made in favour of the Company by the previous Government, and by the Congress assembled during that Government, were binding, or whether the new Government and the Congress which it might convoke would repudiate them. These doubts were very soon dispelled by the Government of the President Señor D. Ponciano Leiva, which lost no time in declaring that it was determined to support everything that could tend to the completion of the Railway, and to liberate Honduras from the insupportable engagements which burdened the Republic on account of the loans.

Notwithstanding this declaration, and the praiseworthy intentions manifested by the Government of the President Señor D. Ponciano Leiva, the Inter-oceanic Railway Company found itself entangled in a net of difficulties which prevented its development and consolidation. On the formation of the Company, its promoters, who were the members of the Committee of Investigation appointed by the bondholders at the meeting of January 10th, 1873, reckoned upon the support of the contractors for the previous loans, that is, Messrs. Bishoffsheim and Goldschmidt, Mr. Lefèvre, and Messrs. Dreyfus, Scheyer, and Co. These gentlemen were not willing to support the Company after its formation, to the extent which the Directors of the Company expected they would; from whence arose most serious complaints, complications, and even legal proceedings. On the other hand, the bondholders of Paris began to make complaints against the Company, the result of which was, that many of them combined to take legal proceedings in France, and altogether refused to have anything to do with the said Company. The Directors of the Company had very serious discussions among themselves, and made complaints and accusations against each other, which were rather induced by having to contend with so many mischances than by well-founded reasons. The Special Commissioner of the Honduras Government himself could not escape very serious personal attacks upon questions in which not Dr. C. E. Bernhard personally, but the powers of the Special Commissioner of the Honduras Government were involved, and whether he was or was not proceeding in accordance with law, and as legally representing the interests of the Republic.

Immediately after the meeting of January 10, 1873, two engineers, Messrs. W. A. Brooks and Charles A. Alberga, had been sent to Honduras, to inspect and survey the Railway Line already constructed, as well as the two sections traced out, and to report thereon. Their report, which bears date April 25, 1873, was published in the "Foreign Times" of London on the 12th of July following. Finally, in September, two other engineers, Messrs. Seymour and Huston, also went to Honduras, by order of the Directors of the Interoceanic Railway Company. They were to take measures on the spot to proceed with the construction of fifteen miles of the Railway on account of the Company; but it appears that those gentlemen withdrew without doing anything to show that the works were about to be begun.

While this was going on, the bonds of the Honduras loans, which had not been converted into the Company's shares, went down in price until they were quoted at 6½ per cent.; and all the efforts of the Directors of the Company to inspire confidence and give hope had not the slightest effect in restraining this depreciation.

The Company convoked two meetings of the shareholders in October and November last, to give an account of the difficulties against which it was contending, in consequence of the bulk of the bondholders not having decided to convert their bonds into shares of the said Company, on account of the poor subscription for the preference shares, and because Messrs. Bischoffsheim and Lefèvre refused to give the moral and financial support which they had proffered on the formation of the said Company; but nothing positive was settled at those meetings to relieve the Company from its pressing engagements. On the contrary, those meetings were a fruitful source of bitter recriminations and personal attacks, which were certainly not the best means to meet the great crisis, nor to overcome the enormous difficulties.

The Honduras Government convoked the National Congress to meet at Comayagua, the capital of the Republic, at the end of January, 1875. That Congress was to examine the state of the affairs connected with the Railway, with the loans contracted to construct it, and with the condition of the Company formed to complete it; so that it might, on consideration of the previous proceedings, give the necessary directions and pass definitive resolutions.

For this purpose a delegate of the Company, Mr. John William Atkinson, departed for Comayagua, by way of Omoa, in the steamer which left Southampton on the 17th of December; and the special Commissioner of the Government, Dr. C. E. Bernhard, also left by the same steamer, and with the same destination, to give an account of what he had done in Europe for the last two years, exclusively occupied in directing in some measure, the affairs of the unfortunate Railway.

It is to be hoped that the Congress, in consideration of such difficult circumstances, which cannot be easily remedied, will pass a *vote of confidence* in favour of the President and Government of Honduras, so that such measures shall be taken as, according to circumstances, may be deemed most suitable for the praiseworthy object of rescuing this undertaking.

This is, briefly narrated, the history of the Honduras Railway, from the time when its construction was first attempted up to the present.

XI.

CONCLUSION.

AFTER having suffered such a series of mischances, failures, and difficulties—such an array of obstacles, disappointments, and annoyances—it seems at first sight that the Honduras Inter-oceanic Railway is a project pursued by misfortune, and never to be achieved, because all the combinations to obtain funds for its construction have been exhausted, and all have met with disaster in one way or another.

Fortunately it is not so. Great projects do not perish thus in modern times. They may suffer mishaps, delays, crises, crashes, and all kinds of calamities; but human pride delights in overcoming and surmounting whatever appears most difficult and insuperable; and for this very reason the Honduras Railway, in spite of the misfortunes which have befallen it, is destined to become a reality sooner or later—to unite the two oceans, and to develop the untold wealth of that favoured section of the New World through which it is traced.

We have read carefully and with interest all that has been written concerning the Honduras Railway, and the territory through which it is to pass. More than thirty volumes, pamphlets, reports, and memorials, in various languages, have been published in Europe during the last few years; and they all agree upon the importance of this great work, and the natural riches of the Honduras territory. We have ourselves seen those riches, in a delicious climate, in a picturesque country, which only requires hands to work and roads for communication, to convert it into an emporium of production and commerce. But what has attracted our attention most is the very important "Report," in 102 printed folio pages, presented by Mr. Squier, in the year 1859, to the Directors of the Company which was then formed in London, and which broke down under the circumstances mentioned in the first Chapter. That Report—founded on the information of first-class engineers, and other experienced men and travellers worthy of entire credit, and on actual surveys and observations on the spot—gives a most complete and favourable idea of the Line, of the sea-ports at each end of it, of the climate and resources of Central America, and of the practicability of the Line without other than the most ordinary difficulties which are met with in every undertaking of this kind.

There can be no doubt as to the magnificent forests of Honduras—these are well known to everyone by their valuable timber; but the interior of the country is not so well known, with its millions of pines of enormous dimensions, which must in time give rise to immense trade and employment in the exportation of timber, the extraction of resin, turpentine, and other products. Nor can there be any doubt of the mineralogical riches of Honduras, especially its gold-washings and inexhaustible mines of silver and copper. Neither can there be any question as to the fertility of the country, of its excellent climate, favourable for European immigration, agriculture, and cattle breeding.

What has been doubted by some people who are not acquainted with those regions, is the practicability of the Line; and we are therefore about to conclude this Pamphlet by giving the official statements, obtained from the surveys of the Engineers, and well attested. They show that the construction of the Honduras Inter-oceanic Railway need not meet with any particular or extraordinary obstacle that can even be considered as a difficulty of an average character.

The highest point which the Honduras Railway has to pass is 2956 feet above the level of the sea; and that will be reduced to 2926 by a cutting to be made at that height. The point referred to is at a distance of 165 miles from the Atlantic, and 68 miles from the Pacific.

The gradients of the Line meet at that culminating point; but the disposition of those gradients is favourable to the direction and the kind of traffic for which the Line is to be used.

The following Table will show the importance of these gradients for the whole length of the Railway.

	Sections.	Distance.	Gradient.
1. From	Port Cortez to Mauricios	67 miles	2.83 feet
2. ,,	Mauricios to Ojos de Agua	40 ,,	21.27 ,,
3. ,,	Ojos de Agua to Ilampa	23 ,,	29.21 ,,
4. ,,	Ilampa to Rio Grande	26 ,,	20.12 ,,
5. ,,	Rio Grande to Rancho Chiquito	9 ,,	84.50 ,,
6. ,,	Rancho Chiquito to San Antonio	22½ ,,	95.00 ,,
7. ,,	San Antonio to Caridad	5½ ,,	48.72 ,,
8. ,,	Caridad to the Bay of Fonseca	40 ,,	13.50 ,,
	Total	233 miles	25.33 feet

The steepest gradient is from San Antonio to Rancho Chiquito, but that may be reduced by making some slight variations in the track.

The works to be done throughout the Honduras Interoceanic Railway, with the materials and labour, are calculated as follows :—

LINE FROM PORT CORTEZ TO THE BAY OF FONSECA.
(233 *miles of Railway*.)

Class of Work.	Quantities.	Estimate.
Excavation in rock . . .	4,457,000 cubic yds.	4,457,000 dols.
„ earth. . .	1,712,000 „ „	342,400 „
Embankment	8,496,000 „ „	2,127,000 „
Tunnels	59,700 „ „	298,500 „
Masonry of all kinds . .	272,149 „ „	1,204,440 „
Bridges	6,120 feet run	367,200 „
Ballast	451,605 cubic yds.	451,605 „
Sleepers, rails, &c. . . .	235¼ miles	2,355,000 „
Water stations, workshops, &c.	...	267,000 „
Piers	...	60,000 „
Preparatory road . . .	231 miles	570,000 „
Professional services . .	...	500,000 „
Contingencies	10 per cent.	1,304,334 „
Cost per mile { 62,110 dollars.* £12,242.	Total cost { 14,347,679 dols. £2,869,000.	

On examination of the above particulars it will be clearly seen that there is no insuperable obstacle or difficulty in the way of the possible construction of the Honduras Railway. The only difficulty is to obtain the estimated funds for the completion of the work.

If the bondholders in London and Paris understood their real interests, they would at once subscribe the necessary capital, in proportion to the bonds which they hold; and with that capital, strictly administered, the Line might be finished

---

* *Author's Note.*—This estimate appears very much exaggerated. The line can be completed, including the necessary rolling stock, at the rate of £9,000 per mile.

in two years, and thus all the immense interests would be secured.

At present the bonds of the Honduras loans are quoted in the European Exchanges at 6½ per cent., which is as much as to say that the whole of them are not worth a great deal more than £450,000 in the market, for they could be bought for that sum. Well, then, the part of the Railway already constructed is worth about double that sum; and the concessions made by the Government in favour of the Company for constructing the Railway are worth, without exaggeration, twenty times that sum, if they are properly managed. If every bondholder would subscribe 30 per cent. more in cash upon the nominal value of the bonds in his possession, the Railway would be finished, and it would be the property of the said bondholders; the concessions of the Government would be turned to account, and would be a source of immense riches; the bondholders would then have no reason to complain of former disasters and damages, and the Honduras Government would see its wishes fulfilled in the endowment of the Republic with an Inter-oceanic Railway which would afford a solid basis for the development and utilization of its natural riches.

Certainly it is difficult, exceedingly difficult, to convince all and each of the bondholders, by serious calculations, of what they ought to do for the protection of their own interests, and to extricate themselves from the ruin into which they have fallen. It is certain, also, that many of the bondholders have not the means of advancing 30 per cent. more in cash on the nominal value of their bonds. Nevertheless, in regard to the first expedient, it has never been attempted in any way—perhaps no idea of attempting it has ever been entertained; and yet, if the attempt were made, it might produce favourable results. In regard to the second, those who really cannot afford the extraordinary addition of 30 per cent. to the bonds which they possess, have three resources:—1. To keep their bonds, in order to assert their rights in future, if there should be an opportunity. 2. To sell them at the quotation price. 3. To sell a part of them for the purpose of providing the extraordinary addition of 30 per cent. on the nominal value of those which they retain.

The great difficulty—or rather the great necessity, if such an operation is to be made practicable—is to know how to combine, to introduce, to explain, and to carry it out; to examine in due time, without exaggeration or depreciation, its inconveniences and its advantages; to smooth down the former beforehand by foresight and practical remedies, and to make the latter available by energy and activity.

Messrs. Bischoffsheim and Goldschmidt, Dreyfus, Scheyer, and Co., and Mr. Lefèvre, are the men who ought to bring about an effective combination; and they would certainly succeed, if they took pains, and procured the aid of efficient administrators, able professional men, honourable contractors for the material works of the Railway, and practical, energetic and active persons, exclusively devoted to the purpose of developing the value of the Government concessions and turning them to account, by promoting emigration, working the mines, cutting timber, and other lucrative occupations.

This great enterprise of the Honduras Railway has engaged the attention of many, too many, speculators, stockjobbers, intruders, busy critics, officials indifferent to the fate of Honduras, intriguers, and others whom we must not mention; but, on the other hand, it has always wanted a competent man for an enterprise rendered most difficult and complicated by the circumstances which surrounded it—a man alike theoretical and practical, financier and engineer, contractor and director—equally capable of discussing financial plans and combinations with the bankers, and surveys and designs with the engineers—as able to direct and control the accounts as to maintain a strict inspection over the works of the Line and to instruct the workmen in the use of their tools—a man of mental and physical force, with ability to take the lead over all parties, with no other aim than the object proposed, with no other ambition than that of attaining it —a man after the fashion of M. de Lesseps, who would know what to do in any unforeseen contingency, whether financial, professional, or practical.

Mr. Squier, who conceived the idea of the Railway, is the man who most nearly approaches this type. He proposed the problem with intelligence and industry; but he was unfortunate—he lacked material support and good health. The last Trustees in London, Messrs. G. B. Kerferd, Edward Haslewood, and Captain Bedford Pim, undertook the trust, and received it from their predecessors when the enterprise was given over and expiring. The first two represented the integrity of commerce and the Exchange, the last was characterized by enthusiasm and energetic will; but the difficulties were already beyond their abilities and their means of action. The Special Commissioner, Dr. Bernhard, was a pattern of an industrious and indefatigable man; but, after two years of constant labour and arrangements, he found out that he had to do with people who trusted much more to their own projects and to chance, than to substantial and well-considered plans. And, finally, the Minister in London, Señor Gutierrez, represents good faith, disinterestedness, and the spirit of conciliation. He has frequently been the victim sacrificed on one side for the interests of the Railway and of his country, and on the other for the complaints of the bondholders and the difficulties in Europe.

But it is a manifest injustice to require that this public man should be able, and ought to serve at the same time interests so opposed and heterogeneous—to obey the instructions of his Government, to arrange differences and quarrels, to examine and correct professional projects, to instruct the bankers, check the accounts, avoid ruinous operations on 'Change, foresee the consequences of political revolutions, do business with usurers, pay the bondholders, give publicity to events, maintain the reserve required by his diplomatic position, counsel the unwary not to meddle with hazardous operations, maintain credit, pay the dividends, finish the Railway,—and all this, as well as many various exigencies on all sides, without any other aid than officious criticism from some, and empirical advice from others.

Of course, the representative of a foreign country, whoever he may be, looks after the interests of his country, and gives it an account of his official acts; but it would be ridiculous for him to pretend to advise, in a foreign and essentially speculating country, upon the risks which are run by investing capital in usurious transactions, or in speculations on 'Change without judgment.

Messrs. Bischoffsheim and Goldschmidt, Dreyfus, Scheyer, and Co., and Lefèvre, were the contractors for the loans. Under the auspices of the first two firms, the bonds were offered to the English and French public, and bought by the present holders (at whatever price it may have been), not so much on the strength of the guarantees offered by the Republic, as in consideration of the respectability of those firms, and by reason of the efforts which they themselves made to dispose of the bonds. Those bankers, then, are morally bound to come to the aid of the Honduras Government, by devising a substantial combination for the completion of the Railway, to rescue the many sacrifices which have already been made, and the considerable part of the Railway already constructed, from utter failure, and the interests both of the bondholders and of the Honduras Government from complete destruction. Were they to do so, they would nobly respond to what their honour and credit require, and to what the bondholders and the Honduras Government have a right to expect; and they themselves, by resolving, at a time of peril, to undertake once more the provision for the Railway, would reap the desired returns from a grand enterprise which, when in danger, will have been rescued by the support and energy of two respectable banking houses, which are firmly determined to carry it out and succeed in their purpose.

APPENDIX

TO THE

ENGLISH EDITION.

No. I.

OFFICIAL DOCUMENTS.

LEGISLATIVE ADVERTISEMENT.

Comayagua, 30th May, 1868.

The President of the Republic of Honduras to the Inhabitants thereof.

NOTICE is hereby given: That the Sovereign Congress of the Republic, after examination of the documents transmitted to the Supreme Executive Power from the Legation in London, concerning the Loan intended for the construction of the Honduras Inter-oceanic Railway, and those relating to the execution of that work by the Contractor, William MacCandlish,

DECREES: Sole Article.—The Contract No. 1, and the additional agreements concerning the construction of the said Line, are approved throughout.

Given at the Sessions Hall, Comayagua, the 18th of February, 1868.

JUAN LOPEZ, Deputy, President.
CARLOS MADRID, Deputy, Secretary.
JERONIMO ZELAYA, Deputy, Secretary.

To the Executive Power.—THEREFORE, let this be executed.

JOSE MARIA MEDINA.

TRINIDAD FERRARI, Minister for Foreign Affairs.

Comayagua, 29th February, 1868.

LEGISLATIVE ADVERTISEMENT.

Comayagua, 30th May, 1868.

Authorizing the Executive Power to organise the working of the Mines on account of the State.

The President of the Republic of Honduras to the
Inhabitants thereof.

NOTICE is hereby given: That the Sovereign Congress of the Republic, considering that the Government ought to work the National Mines, as one of the means to be applied to the redemption of the Loan which is to be employed for the construction of the Honduras Inter-oceanic Railway; in the exercise of its powers,

DECREES: Article 1.—The Supreme Executive Power is authorized to regulate and organize on account of the State the working of the National Mines in the circle of Aramecina, and which cannot be claimed by private persons.

Art. 2.—Within six months from the publication of this law, the Government shall specify the abandoned Mines in the Republic which are to be worked on account of the State, and within that period no claim to an abandoned Mine shall be allowed.

Given at Comayagua, in the Sessions Hall of the National Congress, on the 24th of February, 1868.

JUAN LOPEZ, Deputy, President.
CARLOS MADRID, Deputy, Secretary.
JERONIMO ZELAYA, Deputy, Secretary.

To the Executive Power: THEREFORE, let this be executed.

JOSE MARIA MEDINA.

TRINIDAD FERRARI, Minister of the Interior.

Comayagua, 28*th February*, 1868.

LEGISLATIVE ADVERTISEMENT.

Comayagua, 15*th April*, 1872.

DECREE, No. 15.

The President of the Republic of Honduras to the
Inhabitants thereof.

NOTICE is hereby given: That the Sovereign Congress of

the Republic, having before it the Government Decree of 4 December, 1870, which ratifies the Agreement concluded in London on the 17th of July of the same year by Señor D. Carlos Gutierrez, Minister Plenipotentiary to Her Britannic Majesty, duly authorized by the Government to negotiate a Loan of £2,500,000 sterling nominal value, intended for the completion of the Honduras Railway, on the one part, and Mr. Henry Louis Bischoffsheim and Goldschmidt, on the other part,

DECREES: Sole Article.—The aforesaid Decree is approved throughout. Given at Comayagua, in the Sessions Hall of the National Congress, on the 20th of February, 1872.

MANUEL COLINDRES, Deputy, President.
PEDRO FERNANDEZ, Deputy, Secretary.
ESTEVAN FERRARI, Deputy, Secretary.

To the Executive Power.—THEREFORE, let this be executed.

JOSE MARIA MEDINA.

VALENTINE DURON, Minister for Public Works, &c.

Comayagua, 23rd *February*, 1872.

DECREE, No. 17.

The President of the Republic of Honduras to the Inhabitants thereof.

NOTICE is hereby given: That the Sovereign Congress of the Republic, having before it the Government Decree of 4th August, 1871, which ratifies the Agreement concluded on the 21st of April of the same year between Sr D. Carlos Gutierrez, Minister of the Republic of Honduras to Her Britannic Majesty, and Messrs. Bishoffsheim and Goldschmidt, concerning the bonds of the Paris Loan of 1869,

DECREES: Sole Article.—The said Decree is approved throughout.

Given at Comayagua, in the Sessions Hall of the National Congress, on the 20th of February, 1872.

MANUEL COLINDRES, Deputy, President.
ESTEVAN FERRARI, Deputy, Secretary.
PEDRO FERNANDEZ, Deputy, Secretary.

To the Executive Power.—THEREFORE, let this be executed.

JOSE MARIA MEDINA.

VALENTIN DURON,
Minister of the Interior, of Public Works, &c.

Comayagua, 23rd *February*, 1872.

DECREE, No. 18.
The President of the Republic of Honduras to the Inhabitants thereof.

NOTICE is hereby given: That the Sovereign Congress of the Republic, having before it the Government Decree of 7th August, 1871, which ratifies the Agreement concluded in London on the 21st of April of the same year, between Sr D. Carlos Gutierrez, Minister of Honduras to Her Britannic Majesty, and Mr. Charles Lefèvre, concerning the payment and advance of certain sums of pounds sterling, which have taken place on account of the Honduras Inter-oceanic Railway,

DECREES: Sole Article.—The aforesaid Decree is approved throughout.

Given at Comayagua, in the Sessions Hall of the National Congress, on the 20th of February, 1872.

MANUEL COLINDRES, Deputy, President.
ESTEVAN FERRARI, Deputy, Secretary.
PEDRO FERNANDEZ, Deputy, Secretary.

To the Executive Power.—THEREFORE, let this be executed.

JOSE MARIA MEDINA.

VALENTIN DURON,
Minister for the Home Department and for Public Works &c.

Comayagua, 23rd *February*, 1872.

Republic of Honduras.—Ministry of Foreign Affairs.

Comayagua, 29 *December*, 1873.

" SIR,—

I have the pleasure of inclosing to you herewith a copy of the Decree by which the Sovereign Congress of the Republic ratifies the approval given by the Provisional Government to the Contract concluded by you and the Commissioner Bernhard with the Honduras Inter-oceanic Railway Company Limited, for the construction of the Inter-oceanic Railway of this Republic.

As you will see by the above-mentioned Decree, the Supreme Congress only requires that the Contract in question shall be duly executed, and that all the formalities and requirements prescribed for such documents by the English laws shall be observed and fulfilled, so that the said Contract may become a State document.

You, then, in concurrence with Mr. Bernhard, will take all such proceedings with the Company as are necessary, and adapted to obtain, in regard to the formalities of its execution, all the proper securities for its validity as understood in the approval granted by this Government, previously communicated to you, and in the subsequent ratification of the Sovereign Congress, which I now forward to you duly attested.

I am, M. le Ministre,
Your very obedient Servant,
JEREMIAS CISNEROS.

Señor Don Carlos Gutierrez,
Minister of Honduras, London.

Inclosure in the above Letter.

Republic of Honduras.—Ministry for Foreign Affairs.

The President of the Republic of Honduras to
the Inhabitants thereof.

NOTICE is hereby given: That the Sovereign Constituent Congress has decreed as follows:

The Sovereign Constituent National Congress of the Republic,

Considering that the fresh negotiations entered into by the Minister Plenipotentiary Señor Don Carlos Gutierrez and the Special Commissioner, Dr. Don C. E. Bernhard, with the Limited Company for the construction of the Honduras Inter-oceanic Railway Company remove the great difficulties presented by the system adopted for the completion of that undertaking; and considering that they tend to promote one of the greatest interests of the Republic, the Assembly, with the respective documents before it,

DECREES: Art. 1.—The Contract concluded in London, on the 12th day of July of the present year, by the aforesaid Messrs. Gutierrez and Bernhard, with the Limited Company, is approved, on the same terms as it was approved by the Provisional Government of the Republic, for the continuation and completion of the works of the Inter-oceanic Railway.

Art. 2.—In order that the aforesaid Contract may have full effect, and Honduras be bound to the Contracting Company, it is indispensable that the members of the latter should authorize the deed of the aforesaid Contract by the signatures of their legal representatives, in the form and according to the regulations prescribed by the laws of Great Britain for the execution and fulfilment of Contracts of this nature.

Given at Comayagua, in the Sessions Hall of the National Constituent Congress, on the 24th of December, 1873.

R. MIDENCE, Deputy, President.
F. HERNANDEZ, Deputy, Secretary.
PEDRO RIVERA BUSTILLO, Deputy, Secretary.

THEREFORE, let this be promulgated and printed.

CELEO ARIAS.

JEREMIAS CISNEROS, Minister for Foreign Affairs.

Comayagua, *December* 25, 1873.

A true copy.

Comayagua, *December,* 29, 1873.

CISNEROS.

No. II.

CUTTING THE TIMBER AND WORKING THE MINES IN HONDURAS, TO APPLY THE PROCEEDS IN PART PAYMENT OF THE DIVIDENDS OF THE LOANS CONTRACTED IN EUROPE FOR THE CONSTRUCTION OF THE INTER-OCEANIC RAILWAY.

When the first loan was contracted for with the firm of Messrs. Bischoffsheim, Goldschmidt, & Co., in 1867, for the construction of the Inter-oceanic Railway, the Supreme Government issued a Decree appointing a Board of Works under the denomination of "National Committee of Honduras," for the purpose of proceeding with certain funds assigned to the Government in the Contract itself, to cut mahogany and other timber, and to work some of the rich mines which there are in the country, and to develope other branches of industry, in order to remit the proceeds to Messrs. Bischoffsheim & Goldschmidt, the Government Agents in London.

The said "National Committee" was composed of men of reputation and honour, such as D. Francisco Alvarado, D. Manuel Colindres, D. Ramon Valenzuela, D. Céleo Arias, and others of similar position. They made the greatest efforts to discharge the duties imposed on them by the Government in order to send the proceeds to London. On the other hand, the Government entered into contracts with Messrs. Debrot of Omoa, Morris and Co. of Amapala, and another firm at Belize, to cut timber and send it to Europe; whilst mining engineers and overseers were sent out from London to undertake some of the principal works of the various mines about Aramecina. But before the fruits of these efforts could be reaped, the Government received information that some of the bills drawn against the funds placed at its disposal for this purpose in London had been protested, because the bonds of the loans could not be sold so fast as was necessary; and this, together with political disturbances in the country, was the reason that the Government was unable to send to London the timber and minerals which had been announced to its representatives, and which were to have been consigned to Messrs. Bischoffsheim and Goldschmidt.

The engineers who went to Honduras to commence the mining operations in the neighbourhood of Amapala, were Messrs. Mauduit, Emmerson, and Mercer.

Here follows the decree of the Honduras Government dissolving the "National Committee"; it was published in the Official Gazette of June 14, 1870.

"SUPREME DECREE OF 28 MAY, 1870.

"José Maria Medina, Captain-General and President of the Republic.

"WHEREAS, the National Committee having suspended its drafts upon the funds in London and Paris, on account of the difficulty of getting the Bills of Exchange paid, this Board, which was organised to negotiate, has no further purpose. As I wish to reconcile economy in expense with the indispensable security in the management of those funds,

"I DECREE: Article 1.—The National Committee, created by decree of the 2nd of May last, for the management of the funds negotiated for undertakings in the Republic, is dissolved; but the contracts made by that Board remain, just as if they had been concluded with the Government.

"Art. 2.— A Special Treasurer is appointed for the administration of those funds; he is to have the same qualifications and to give the same security as are required by Art. 47 of the Treasury Law for a Treasurer General. His salary is to be 1,000 dollars a year; he will have a clerk with a salary of 240 dollars, and an office as may be necessary.

"Art. 3.—The Committee will proceed to liquidate and present its accounts to the Minister of Finance, according to the regulations; and will deliver what it has in hand, with the goods and chattels, to the Treasurer, as soon as it receives notice of his appointment and acceptance of office.

"Art. 4.—The Treasurer will keep his accounts in the same book as the Committee, will compare the items with the orders of the Treasury, balance the cash monthly, and render his account to the Ministry of Finance for the approval of the Government.

"Art. 5.—Any bills that are hereafter to be drawn, will be drawn by the Ministry for Foreign Affairs, as they were before the appointment of the Committee.

"Art. 6.—Let this be communicated to the Ministers of Honduras in London and Paris, and to any one else whom it may concern; and the Ministers of Finance and of Foreign Affairs are charged with the execution of this Decree.

"Given at Gracias, the 28th of May, 1870.

"JOSE MARIA MEDINA.

"FRANCISCO ALVARADO, Minister of Finance."

No. III.

APPENDIX TO THE REPORT OF THE COMMITTEE APPOINTED BY THE HONDURAS BONDHOLDERS AT THEIR MEETING ON THE 10TH OF JANUARY, 1873.*

No. 1.

4, Westminster Chambers, Victoria Street, S.W.;
January 18th, 1873.

YOUR EXCELLENCY,

I have the pleasure to enclose a print of certain Resolutions passed at a General Meeting of the Honduras Bondholders, held at the London Tavern on the 10th instant, and respectfully to ask that, in conformity therewith, you will be good enough to furnish

* See page 51.

the Committee of Investigation with the particulars of the Loans made by the Honduras Government, the amount realized thereon, and the disposition thereof, or the names and addresses of the persons from whom the particulars can be obtained; and also any further information which you may think necessary to enable the Committee to carry out the terms of the Resolutions passed at the Meeting.

‘ As the Committee meet again on Tuesday next, and are anxious not to delay their duties, they will be obliged if you will reply before that date.   I am, Sir, &c.,

CHAIRMAN OF THE COMMITTEE.

To their Excellencies,
    Don Carlos Gutierrez, London; and
    Don Victor Herran, Paris.

No. 2.

Potrerillos Station (three miles South of the River Venta, or Santiago, and 59 miles from Puerto Caballos);
December 2nd, 1872.

Dear Captain BEDFORD PIM,—

The *Belize* steam-ship was put into quarantine on its arrival at Belize, because there had been one or two cases of small-pox in the interior of Jamaica; and I was, therefore, detained at Belize until the return of the schooner from Omoa, in which schooner (the *Puerto Caballos*) I sailed for Omoa on the 16th ult.; but on arriving off the coast of the State of Honduras, I had the good luck of a heavy south-wester springing up, which compelled the master to change his course for the noble harbour of Puerto Caballos. On the 23rd ult. I left by the morning train for San Pedro, and thence to the terminus of the first section at the river Venta, or Santiago, 56 miles distant from Puerto Caballos. We went at the rate of twenty-five miles an hour; but the condition of the Railway would have safely afforded a rate of forty miles an hour. The works on the line of Railway had been respected by the adverse parties in the late intestine troubles, during which a considerable quantity of mahogany, cedar, and dye-woods were sent down the line. The agent of Mr. Debrot, the British Vice-Consul of Omoa, came up the line in the same carriage with me, and told me that Mr. Debrot had already sent down the Railway for shipment at Puerto Caballos this year about 1,300,000 cubic feet of mahogany, besides a large quantity of rosewood, fustic, and other dye-woods, and that he was making arrangements for sending down the line next year 3,000,000 cubic feet of mahogany; and he (the agent) was satisfied that the timber sent by Mr. Debrot alone would maintain the line already made, by the amount of dues paid for the use of the Railway. Above 200 mules are daily employed in conveying goods from the present terminus of the Railway, 56 miles from the port, to the city of Comayagua, and also to Tegucigalpa. This traffic will vastly increase the progress of the Inter-oceanic Railway further to the southward on the second section. I have carefully examined the plan and sections of the first district of the second section, which is of exceedingly easy construction; the cuttings and embankments for $2\frac{3}{4}$ miles of it are already executed. I have also, during the past week, been as far as Bajo Grande, three leagues south of Azufral, or 83 miles from Puerto Caballos, and am prepared to advise the immediate rapid completion of the bridge over the Venta, and the completion of the Railway to Las Lagunetas, a distance of rather more than 14 miles, which can easily be made available for railway traffic by eight or nine months' work, and enable a further vast quantity of valuable timber to be brought down the line.

I have not had time to estimate the cost of the timber bridge over the Venta, which will be 450 feet in length; but Mr. Innes says that he can readily procure enough in a month for its construction; and, owing to the advantage of the convenience afforded for getting the timber from the forests on each side of the 56 miles of the existing Railway, this is a work which can be cheaply executed, under the immediate superintendence of the Engineer of the first or 56-mile section. There is a large stock of plant on the ground, and about 300 mules and 60 oxen. Thirty of the mules went off to Comayagua with goods, which had just come by the Railway. The traffic along the Railway is already so considerable, that it is high time for the bondholders to have the benefit of the profit for carrying the goods.

I am,
Yours very truly,
W. A. BROOKS.

Potrerillos Station (three miles to the southward of the
River Venta, or Santiago, or 59 miles from Puerto Caballos);
December 2nd, 1872.

Dear CAPTAIN PIM,

Mr. —— has expressed to me his desire to contract with you for the formation of a portion of the line of Railway, being the commencement of the second section; and, after much discussion, I sketched out a letter or tender, which that gentleman has copied and signed, and it is now enclosed. You will see the importance of the immediate progress of this work, which I am satisfied can and will be executed in the time named. The extra quantity of timber which will be brought down the line in the next two years will pay for the construction of these 14 miles and 1,480 feet. You will remember how strongly I insisted upon the paying capabilities of the line, independent of any inter-oceanic traffic, and the amount of timber now being sent down the line proves the soundness of my opinion. Messrs. Guild & Co., of Belize, and other parties, have a large number of men engaged also in getting out mahogany and other valuable woods; and their united forces will be fully equal to Mr. Debrot's, from whose works we may depend upon having 3,000,000 cubic feet of mahogany and rosewood come down the line. The rosewood trees which I saw at Puerto Caballos were magnificent specimens of timber, 16 and 18 inches in diameter. A large French barque was lying in the harbour laden with mahogany, ready for sea, and a Norwegian barque of about 600 tons register came into port the day before I left. On the night previous to my arrival at Puerto Caballos we had a "Norther," which came on suddenly, and drove a large French barque upon the beach of the Ulua River, smashing her in less than a quarter of an hour into pieces not bigger than a table, according to the statement made to me by the mate, who walked, with seven of the crew, from the Ulua to Puerto Caballos. I think it of such importance that these 14 miles of Railway should be forthwith completed, that I advise your acceptance of the tender made by Mr. ———. The works consist of a number of small cuts and embankments, with which I could easily execute and complete the line within six months, if there were sufficient rails, &c., on the ground. I believe there are only about three miles of rails at Puerto Caballos, which can be at once transferred to this work. I recommend you to take the tender to my experienced friend Mr.———, and ask him to examine it, and make such alterations or additions as he may think advisable, remembering that the tender was sketched out by me in great haste. Mr. ——— is agreeable to put down any other pattern of rails, if you can get them more readily than those now used. It will take about 80 tons of rails. I think it of so much consequence to the Bondholders that this work should be proceeded with, that I do not hesitate to advise you personally to enter into an immediate contract to execute these 14 miles and 1,480 feet, including the supply of all rails, &c., you employing Mr. ——— to execute the works tendered for by him; the difference between the amount of his tender, added to the cost of the rails, &c., being a security to you for extra works such as those referred to in Mr. ———'s tender and schedule of prices for them. You will see that I have provided for other contracts going on, which will open out nearly five-sixths of the Railway, leaving the larger cuts to be executed in the period of two years, and making a temporary road for mules to convey the goods and passengers from one line of Railway to another until the whole line is completed. I shall return to Puerto Caballos in time to meet Mr. Alberga, and go with him over the whole of the line to Amapala.

I am, yours very truly,
W. A. BROOKS.

Potrerillos, 59 miles from Puerto Caballos;
December 3rd, 1873.

Dear CAPTAIN BEDFORD PIM,

Yesterday I sent a long letter addressed to No. 4, Westminster Chambers, which will arrive at your hands by this mail. Last year three ships lying off the bar of the Ulua, for the purpose of taking in cargoes of mahogany, were totally wrecked, and this year two have also been wrecked. Two barques are now comfortably taking in their cargoes in the harbour of Puerto Caballos. In order to induce all ships to come to Puerto Caballos, I am sure you will agree with me that the following advertisement, to be inserted in the *Shipping and Mercantile Gazette,* will promote the welfare of the State of Honduras and its bondholders:—

"Notice to Shippers of Spanish Mahogany, &c., from Puerto Caballos, in the State of Honduras.—All ships taking in their cargoes of mahogany and other timber or produce, brought along the Honduras Inter-oceanic Railway, will have their ballast taken out at the steam-crane ballast wharf, free of all charges. Ships of any tonnage can lie alongside of the wharf, as there is a depth of water of 30 feet at all times."

The ballast can be taken out for sixpence a ton, which is a trifle compared to the tonnage got from the mahogany which comes along the line of railway, and the ballast is much wanted to form foundations for the houses and streets of Puerto Caballos. I have already planned the new town in such a manner that a single locomotive will be able to pass continuously along all the principal streets. I have done this upon a scale of 100 feet to the inch.

Directions should also be at once given to the engineer at Puerto Caballos to build a framework beacon, or lighthouse, of 80 feet in height, at the western extremity of the neck of land which forms the harbour. This will cost little, as there is plenty of timber to be got alongside of the Railway.

At English Kay, the entrance to Belize harbour, they have only two ship's lanterns run up to the top of a mast. You will want a good beacon, however, which can be seen when the high land of the coast three miles south of the beacon is covered with mist, or invisible, as I found it.

A very large sum of money can be raised by the sale of the townland building sites. I shall have all this fully prepared for you on your arrival, and some other harbour works, independent of the report on the Railway, by my colleague and myself. This beacon is purely a work which ought to be executed at the expense of the Government; but if there is not money to be got for it, I would erect it, on being remunerated by a grant of land up the country. It is so important to have this beacon properly erected, that I trust you will not think I have erred if I press its formation on the Government when Mr. Alberga and myself are in Comayagua.

I am, Yours very truly,
W. A. BROOKS.

P.S.—I shall send this off by the schooner which sails to meet the *Belize* steamship with the mail from England (and I hope Mr. Alberga), for fear a "norther" should come on and prevent the possibility of the return of the schooner to Belize with answers to letters brought by the mail from England.

Mr. Bain has just shown me a list of the stores. The preparations for the works have been very great, even to articles which I did not expect to meet, such as levels and theodolites, and 10 of *Chubb's iron safes*, on the 2nd section of the line; and 160 houses at various places. There is a great deal which will account for a large expenditure over and above the £8,000 per mile.

No. 3.

GENTLEMEN,—

In accordance with the desire of the Committee, I have the pleasure of stating, to the best of my belief, the means and resources of Honduras. The principal income of the Government is derived from duties paid on imports of merchandise, and some export duties. There is the tariff of 30 per cent. more or less on certain classes of merchandise *ad valorem*, though taken on the gross weight, in the following manner: When the amount to be paid is $100, you pay 40 per cent. in coin, 35 per cent. in Government paper (worth about 40 per cent. in coin), and 25 per cent. in liquidations—that is, in paper issued by the Government to officers in the army, which represents sometimes one-half or one-third, or even only one-quarter of the nominal worth.

The value of the import of foreign merchandise in the three seaports of the Republic, and (very little) by the land frontiers of the neighbouring states, is about $1,500,000. It is proposed now that the duties on the merchándise should be paid in coin, but reducing them from 30 to 25 per cent., being the same rate as is paid in Salvador; this would give the Government a clear income of $375,000. Out of this would have to be paid $120,000 for interest yearly on the floating debt, which will be consolidated in a 6 per cent. interest-bearing paper, and $27,000 for paying interest and sinking fund for the small loan of £90,000, which is secured upon the Custom Duties of Amapala, and which loan results out of the settlement of the old Federal debt of 1827. The rest—and what the Government gets out of the sale of stamped paper, with duties on the exportation of raw silver, the monopoly on tobacco, duty on slaughtering cattle, total $100,000—would give to the Government a very comfortable income of about $260,000, being $100,000 more than it now has.

Gold mines in quartz, or wash gold in rivers, are to be found, but not in any sufficient quantity to be worked alone. Gold is to be obtained from the silver ores, as most of the silver ores contain gold. Silver mines are to be found in nearly all parts of the Cordilleras, and have been worked by the Spaniards; and I can assure you that not one-third of these mines have been worked, or even claimed. There exist silver mines in and around Aramacina and Caridat, the second and third towns on the Railroad from the Pacific coast. A little further on, in the district of the Indians, near Curaren, rich silver mines are worked. The Indians themselves continually find gold containing silver, and bring it to market, but never show their workings, and jealously prevent any one seeing their mines. You will therefore comprehend how rich such mines must be, when people without any knowledge, implements, or machinery annually bring for sale 5,000 or 8,000 marcs. The emigration and the Railroad will bring all these mines into the hands of the people. There are rich silver mines yielding a good profit on the north and north-east side of Tegucigalpa; every year the people there find more veins. On the north-east of Comayagua are others, one of which the Government has begun to work without much effect, from want of knowledge. Other mines, of world-wide fame, are in the department of Cholutaca (below the town of Corpus), and in the department of Jus'c'uaran or El Paraiso.

I consider the copper mines of Honduras of much more importance than the silver mines. They are always on the surface of the land and

K

go sometimes down to a depth of 100 yards, and yet there is not one of them really worked. When copper coin was made in Honduras, they took the metal where they could get it best from the surface. The surface copper is often mixed with iron and tin, and it is only necessary to melt the sulphate and oxide of copper, and coin it. Such deposits are to be found in the departments of La Victoria (Nacaome), Comayagua, Gracias, Tegucigalpa, Choluteca, Jus'c'uaran; but the greatest attention, I think, is due to one of the largest deposits, lying very near the railroad track of the third section. About fifteen miles from Aramacina Silver Mines, but divided from them by a high ridge of Cordilleras, is a small town of the name of Lugaren, or Alubaren. Coming from the town of Nacaome (40 miles distant), there is a hill called La Questa de los Camerones, about 2,000 or 3,000 feet above the sea, where the road passes over a tract of decayed sulphate of copper. For nearly two miles nothing can be seen but the grey-greenish colour of the decayed copper salt, without any more vegetation than stunted bushes here and there, the atmosphere being impregnated with the salt.

The Timber.—All the north and east coast, far up the rivers running into the Atlantic, has a growth of the largest and finest timber. We may reckon that about 5,000 square miles of the territory are thickly covered by mahogany and other trees of fine timber; which, when properly worked by different gangs, using the rivers for bringing down, and all the numerous inlets of the sea for loading, in four or five years may be got out to the extent at least of five millions of trees. Now, these enterprises must be, and will be, undertaken by private companies, which, when paying only a royalty of eight shillings per tree, will give £2,000,000.

Lands.—Honduras contains 40,000 square miles, of which about 5,000 are in private hands, or town lands. The others are Tierres Vadillas, that is to say, land of which the Government can dispose. The common law is, that any private individual who proves that the lands he desires are free, may take them for cultivation or cattle grazing at a price of $200 in paper bonds of the Government, which generally vary from 40 to 50 per cent. in coin value. One square mile contains about 49 Caballerias. Taking for granted that, from the total area of Honduras, 5,000 square miles are in private hands, and 18,000 are not available on account of sterility—mountains, rivers, lakes, swamps—there are yet 20,000 square miles. Granted that only 2,000 square miles, or 100,000 Caballerias, would be taken when the Railway is finished by speculators; by paying for each Caballeria only £10 in coin, we should have £1,000,000 more at the disposal of the Government. Yours very respectfully,

E. BERNHARD.

No. 4.

Central America has, within the last few years, made rapid progress, and its commerce and resources have been considerably developed. The difficulties and expense of bringing the produce to the coast have, however, in many instances checked, if not completely impeded, the exportation of many articles of low value.

Mahogany, cedar, and other furniture woods are found in abundance, but only in the interior of the country and in the mountainous districts, and the heavy expense of bringing them to the ports of shipment has prevented the expansion of the trade. The present high prices of mahogany have lately induced merchants to turn their attention once again to Honduras and Nicaragua, and a fair amount of export has taken place. It is, however, difficult to over-estimate the amount of wood which might be exported from these countries, should an easy access be provided, and combined with moderate freight.

The growth of sugar and coffee has largely increased, but the former article cannot bear the heavy freights at present ruling over the Isthmus; and the trade is, therefore, principally carried on by sailing vessels. The freight of these vessels is, however, also very high, being on an average £3. 10s. to £3. 15s. or £4 per 20 cwt.; and the time employed in bringing the cargo round the Cape (an average of 5 to 5½ months), the heavy marine insurance, the loss in weight, and the loss of interest on capital employed, may be said to increase the freight by very nearly £1 per ton. This heavy freight, and the difficulty of finding suitable vessels, has diverted much of the trade, and large quantities of sugar find their way to California and the South Pacific ports. These remittances would certainly not take place, should a more reasonable freight be offered; for without doubt the produce would be more easily placed on the European markets, or on that of New York, by taking advantage of the Honduras Interoceanic Railway. Many articles are at present shipped to the United States, and thence re-shipped to Great Britain and the Continent; but there can be no doubt that the proposed Railway would afford a more economical route, and therefore secure the whole of this traffic. Many articles which are not at present exported from Central America, owing to the difficulties and high rates ruling, would no doubt be shipped at a profit, and so considerably increase the returns of the Railway. No positive estimate can be formed of the amount of traffic so stimulated, but I have no hesitation in stating that it would be *considerable* within a very short period; and, as an instance,

I may say that the local traffic created by the 57 miles of rail now in working order, has been far beyond all anticipations; for, although the Line does not as yet pass through any large centre, its earnings will more than cover its working expenses. There seems no doubt that, when the whole Line is opened, the local traffic of Honduras will suffice to pay all the working expenses of the Company; and such trade as may be brought by other countries, and the transit of goods and passengers, will form a good margin of profit.

The States which would furnish the greater traffic are :—

Honduras.—Having at present a population of 600,000 inhabitants, and an extent of 43,000 English square miles.

The principal products are mahogany, cedar, cotton, sugar, tobacco, coffee, and indigo. Its mineral wealth is great; and, should the Railway be completed, this branch of industry would receive a new impulse, and furnish not only employment to many emigrants, but also bring a fair amount of traffic along the Line.

The poorer classes of ores cannot be dealt with in the country, the process being too expensive, and the freights to the coast are so high that they are not exported. There is no doubt that what has happened in Mexico would take place in this country, and that large quantities of mineral stones would be brought to the coast by the Railway, and shipped to England and Germany, where the metal is extracted by a more economical process. Mahogany has of late years been but little exported; the roads are in a wretched condition, and the cost of bringing the wood to the ports is so enhanced that no good result can be anticipated by the exporter. However, since the 57 miles of Railway now completed have been opened to traffic, the export has been resumed; and it has been stated by the engineers and commissioners lately sent out to examine the Line, that the mahogany traffic alone would, if continued on the same scale as at present, suffice to pay the working expenses of the whole Line.

The production of sugar and coffee is but in its infancy in Honduras, only the lands lying most immediately along the coast being available, on account of the want of roads; but the greater part of the country is capable of producing most excellent coffee and good sugar.

Cotton is grown, but on a very small scale, owing to the same circumstances, but it is confidently expected that this would be one of the great sources of income to the Railway. The cotton grown is of good quality, much resembling the "Peruvian," under which denomination it is sold in this country, and obtains high prices.

As stated above, the receipts from the local traffic of Honduras are confidently expected to be amply sufficient to pay all the working expenses of the Line. The incidental receipts from goods and produce brought from other countries would, therefore, form a basis for the calculation of the profits which may be anticipated.

Guatemala.—Population, 1,000,000; area, 15,000 square miles. Produce—coffee, sugar, cochineal, hides, sarsaparilla, mahogany, cedar, and rose-wood. The chief exports are coffee, sugar, cochineal, and hides. Wood is very little exported, owing to the difficulty of bringing it to the port. A Railway is, however, in course of construction to bring the produce to the port at San José (on the Pacific), and this line will bring a considerable amount of goods to the Honduras Railway, this being the shortest and most economical means of placing them in a port of the Atlantic. The production of sugar and coffee has doubled in Guatemala within the last ten years; and the plantations lately made, and still in progress, show that the increase which may be expected within the next ten years will at least be as large.

The production of sugar is also largely increasing in quantity, and the care now bestowed on this branch of agriculture has so much improved the quality that this class of sugar is much sought for in these markets. It is difficult to estimate very accurately the amount of sugar exported from Guatemala, large remittances being made from the smaller ports, in small craft that run along the coast, and take their cargoes to California. This trade will, however, be done away with as soon as the Railway now in construction shall afford an easy access to the port of San José de Guatemala, whence the produce can be shipped per sailing vessels round the Cape, or conveyed in steamers to the Honduras Inter-oceanic Railway, which will convey the cargo to the Atlantic port at almost the same rate of freight as that paid for sailing vessels, and will thus secure a large portion of the traffic. The difficulty in obtaining carts and other means of transport is so great in Guatemala, that in some years (1871 for instance), the cane has been burned, or allowed to rot, sooner than pay the enormous expense of forwarding it to the ports. The freight by steamer, and across the Isthmus of Panama, is at present £5 to £5. 10s. per ton, being 20 per cent. of the value of the sugar on our markets.

The exports of the Sugar are not under	40,000 tons.
,, ,, Coffee about	15,000 ,,
,, ,, Cochineal, Sarza, &c.	10,000 ,,
	65,000 tons.
Total imports	15,000 ,,
Forming together	80,000 tons.

Salvador.—Population, 850,000; 7,230 square miles. Salvador, although the smallest state in Central America, is certainly one of the most important, the activity and industry of the inhabitants having much developed the resources of the country. The principal produce is indigo (of which upwards of £500,000 value is annually exported to Great Britain), sugar, coffee, hides, balsam (called "Balsam of Peru"), tobacco, and some little cotton. The trade is principally carried on by means of steamers connecting with the Panama Railway, but partly also by sailing vessels, the more valuable articles being shipped by the first-named, and the others by the latter means. The freights by steamers are very excessive, being £20 per ton on indigo, £15 on cochineal, £8 per ton on coffee, and £5 to £6 on sugar, &c. Trade is growing rapidly, and facilities of intercourse, combined with more moderate freights, would, without doubt, materially assist the development of the natural resources of the country.

The total exports may be estimated at—

Indigo	1,500 tons
Sugar	20,000 ,,
Coffee	10,000 ,,
Sundries	8,000 ,,

Say in round figures—

Exports	40,000 tons
Imports	20,000 ,,
Forming a total of	60,000 tons.

Costa Rica.— Population, 200,000 inhabitants; area, 16,250 square miles. None of the Central American Republics have made the rapid progress accomplished by Costa Rica within the last ten years. So considerably has the production of coffee increased, that 13,000 tons were shipped to Europe in 1871, and it is estimated that no less than 20,000 tons have been exported in 1872.

The production of sugar, although not increasing in the same proportion, has also been developed, and many new plantations are in course of formation.

The trade of this country may be confidently expected to increase considerably, and it will, without doubt, become one of the most important in Central America. The other productions of the country are hides, iron, coal, and furniture woods; but none of these are extensively produced. The want of roads, and in some cases the difficulty of obtaining labour, have considerably checked these branches of industry. It may, however, be stated that the

Government has lately been able to introduce many reforms, and that the proceeds of the loans granted to the Government have been applied to improvements of the ports, and opening new and good roads, all of which will tend to increase the prosperity of the State. The Railway now in construction between San José (the capital of Costa Rica) and the Port of Punta Arenas (on the Pacific Coast) will also bring further trade in that direction, and will certainly be a great benefit to the Honduras Inter-oceanic Railway.

The total exports of Coffee may be estimated at	20,000 tons
Sugar and other produce	15,000 ,,
	35,000 ,,
To which we must add for the amount of goods imported	10,000 ,,
Thus forming a total of	45,000 tons.

Nicaragua.—Population, 265,000 inhabitants; area, 57,000 square miles.

This country is densely wooded, the most valuable trees being mahogany, rosewood, Nicaragua-wood, cedar, and logwood. It possesses good and extensive pastures, and abundance of cattle. Its principal produce is the sugar-cane, coffee, cocoa, cotton, indigo, and tobacco, all of which are exported. Also ipecacuanha, aloes, sarsaparilla, and many other drugs and medicinal herbs.

One of the principal exports of Nicaragua is also indiarubber, which is found almost all along the coast, and can be shipped at little cost.

The northern parts of the country are rich in minerals; gold, silver, copper, and lead being found. These mines are, however, but inefficiently worked, the principal difficulties consisting in the scarcity of labourers and the expense of transport. The general trade of the country has much increased within the last few years, and the improvement will no doubt continue. It is difficult to estimate very exactly the total amount of the imports and exports of the country. It may, however, be stated that the trade with Europe amounts to—Exports, 35,000 tons; imports, 8,000 tons; forming a total of 43,000 tons.

Beside the trade of the countries above mentioned, the Honduras Inter-oceanic Railway will command a large proportion of the trade now going to the west coast of Mexico by the Panama Railway, and even a certain trade connecting South and Central America with California and China, Japan, and Australia. This trade is at present carried on by means of the Panama Railroad, but the advantages offered by the Honduras route are obvious.

The traffic of the west coast of Mexico is certainly not large, but the trade is steadily increasing; and when produce and goods can be sent to their destination—that is, from the ports of Manhattan, Acapulco, San Blas, Tonalá, &c., to Europe and *vice versâ*—in the space of two months, or even six weeks, instead of three months, now employed by the steamers, or six or seven months required by sailing vessels, there seems no doubt but that the trade will be much increased.

The exports of dye-woods, &c., may be estimated at 12,000 tons to 15,000 tons, and the export of silver and silver coin, on which an *ad valorem* freight is paid, is about $3,000,000.

Many mineral ores are at present not exported, owing to the expensive freight incurred; but should lower rates be established, a a large trade might be profitably carried on.

It has, in the foregoing statement, been shown that the traffic of the several States of Central America is moderately large, and is steadily increasing year by year, as the different branches of industry and agriculture are developed. It should, however, be added, that the three Railways now in course of construction in Honduras, Costa Rica, and Guatemala, will considerably increase the production, and consequently the exportation, of these countries.

It will now be well to direct attention to the probable proportion of this traffic which will be secured to the Honduras Interoceanic Railway, and the consequent revenue derived thereby.

The exports of the four Republics (Honduras traffic being omitted, on the supposition that for the first few years no revenue will be derived from this source, which is said to be sufficient only to pay the working expenses of the Line) have been said to be—

	Exports.	Imports.
Guatemala	65,000 tons	15,000 tons.
Salvador	40,000 ,,	20,000 ,,
Costa Rica	35,000 ,,	10,000 ,,
Nicaragua	35,000 ,,	8,000 ,,
	175,000 tons.	53,000 tons.

Thus forming a total of 238,000 tons, which have to be dealt with.

It has been seen that part of this tonnage is conveyed by sailing vessels, and a part by steamers in connection with the Panama Railroad Company. It is natural to suppose that those articles of low value which cannot at present bear the heavy freights paid for this latter means of conveyance, will still be exported by sailing craft; but it is also certain that the whole of the traffic now carried on by steamers will make use of the Honduras Railway, this line affording not the only advantage of economy, but also less risk and more rapid voyages. It is also probable that the reduction of freight will induce many shippers to send by this route much produce which at present is shipped by sailing vessels, especially when time is an object; and it may also be stated with certainty that *all* importations of the four Republics will cross the Railway which affords the shortest, and therefore most suitable, route for the valuable cargoes of manufactured goods sent to these countries. Only the rough goods (hardware, iron, and such like) will continue to be received by means of sailing vessels; at least, it is not expected that this change can be effected for some years.

Looking at the figures we have to deal with, and the nature of the merchandise which forms them, it can be confidently stated that one half of the outward traffic will pass over the Line, and certainly three-quarters of the importations of the four Republics. Let it, however, be supposed that the Inter-oceanic Railway only secures *one-half* of the natural traffic, some 120,000 tons would be carried over the line, and produce a fair revenue. Let it again be supposed that, to induce the shipment of articles of small value and large bulk, a very low freight is charged, and that the 119,000 *tons* (the *half* of the entire 238,000 tons) carried over the 200 miles of Railway, only produced on an average a freight of 30*s*. per ton (a miserably low figure as compared with the Panama Railway, which charges 83*s*. 6*d*. per ton on the local traffic, and an average of 42*s*. per ton on transit goods running across the Isthmus, which is only forty-two miles in length), the revenue would amount to . £178,000

Another most valuable source of revenue would be the passenger traffic, which in a very short time must become considerable. The population of the five states may be calculated in round figures at 3,000,000, and supposing that only 2½ per cent. of the population travelled by the Line both ways (an excessively small estimate as compared with other countries), and that for the whole length of over 200 miles, the returns only showed an average rate of £2 per head per journey (the charge on the Panama Railroad being £5 for the forty-two miles), this moderate estimate would give 150,000 travellers, and produce . . . 300,000

To this must be added an average of 25,000 foreigners, who would annually avail themselves of the Line, and thus produce (for both journeys) 100,000

Showing a total revenue of £578,000

It will be seen that, in the above estimate, only such portions of the natural traffic as will positively pass over the Line have been taken into consideration. It is certain that a large proportion of the 15,000 tons exported from the southern ports of the west coast of Mexico would be brought across Honduras, as also the greater portion of the importations of the same coast, where some 9,000 tons of fine manufactured goods are received. Other channels would also bring a certain amount of goods and produce, and there can be no doubt that the fact of the completion of the Inter-oceanic Railway would itself greatly increase the present traffic.

Although the same brilliant success cannot be anticipated, it may be stated that the most important lines of railways now existing in the United States were constructed in deserted regions; and there is no reason to believe that the same means and causes would not likewise attract immigration into Honduras, that the vicinity of the Railway track would become populated, that the lands lying on either side of the Line would be cultivated, and that large centres would be formed before long. Of this increase of traffic no estimate can be formed, but experience would lead to the belief that the present prospects of revenue would very shortly be doubled.

G. B. K.

No. IV.

APPENDIX TO THE MEMORANDUM OF ASSOCIATION OF THE HONDURAS INTER-OCEANIC RAILWAY COMPANY LIMITED. *

Issue of Share Capital for conversion.

THE HONDURAS INTER-OCEANIC RAILWAY COMPANY LIMITED.

Incorporated under The Companies Acts, 1862 & 1867.

Issue for Conversion.

The Share Capital of the Company amounts to the sum of £5,347,720, to be represented by the conversion of the Bonds held in the existing Honduras Loans.

29,638	"A." Shares of £100 each	. . .	£2,963,800
8,970	"C." ,, £20 ,,	. . .	179,400

To be exchanged for the outstanding Bonds of the 1867 and 1870 loans.

177,135	"B." Shares of £12 each	. . . .	2,125,620

To be exchanged for the Bonds of the 1869 loan French Issue.

789	"A." Shares of £100 each	. . .	78,900

To be exchanged for the outstanding Bonds of the Federal Debt.

---

* See page 87.

Trustees.

SAMPSON COPESTAKE, Esq. (Messrs. Copestake, Moore, Crampton, & Co.)
Alderman Sir THOMAS WHITE, Ex-Sheriff of London and Middlesex.
(With power to add to their number.)

Directors (pro tem.)
The Committee of HONDURAS BONDHOLDERS.
(Specially re-appointed for the purpose.)

Bankers.
Messrs. GLYN, MILLS, CURRIE, & Co., 67, Lombard Street, E.C.

Auditors.
Messrs. DELOITTEE, DEVER, GRIFFITHS, & Co., 4, Lothbury, London.
Messrs. JAMES & F. FORD, 76 and 77, Cheapside.

Joint-Solicitors.
JOHN TUCKER, Esq., 28, St. Swithin's Lane, London, E.C.
AUGUSTUS BEDDALL, Esq., Baltic Chambers, 108, Bishopsgate St., E.C.

Chief Engineer.
CHARLES SEYMOUR, Esq., M. Inst. C.E. (New York), Chief Engineer of the Madisonville and Bowling Green Railway, the Henderson Nashville Railroad, the Edgefield and Kentucky Railroad, &c. &c.; and formerly Chief of Staff on the Atlantic and Great Western Railroad.

Secretary.
C. F. DENNY, Esq.

Offices.
IN LONDON, 4, Westminster Chambers, Victoria Street, S.W.
IN PARIS, 2, Rue Drouot.

PROSPECTUS.

This Company has been formed for the following purposes:—

1. The acquisition from the Government of Honduras of the Interoceanic Railway, and all its rights, privileges, and interests therein.

2. The acquisition and working of the important concessions hereinafter mentioned.

3. The construction, completion, equipment, and working of the Railway.

GOVERNMENT CONCESSIONS.

The Government of Honduras has granted to this Company the following concessions, which have been confirmed by the existing legislative powers of the State, and take effect immediately:—

A. Such portion of the Line as is already completed, in operation, or in course of construction, together with all stations, houses, buildings, rolling stock, materials, furniture, and equipment.
B. The land necessary for the Line between the Atlantic and Pacific Oceans, with wharves, quays, jetties, landing and navigation rights, &c.
C. The right to import, free from all taxation and import duties, all materials, rolling stock, machinery, stores, and everything required for the making, equipping, working, and maintaining the Railway.
D. The right to construct, maintain, equip, and work the Railway, and levy and take the tolls, rates, and profits of it.
E. All the State lands within a tract of country 10 miles wide, on the course of the Railway, *i.e.*, five miles on each side thereof. This grant is to take effect immediately, as to the first section now in operation, and as to the two remaining sections as the Line is formed.
F. A concession for 99 years of all the antimony, copper, iron, silver, and other mines, including coal and marble, belonging to the State, subject only to the payment of a royalty of ten per cent. on the net profits, after payment of a dividend of ten per cent. on the capital.

The above concessions are accorded by the Honduras Government, in consideration of the present Company protecting the interests of the bondholders of the existing loans on the basis hereinafter proposed.

The Agreement between the Honduras Government and the Company contain, among others, the following important provision: Provided always that, in addition to the privileges of the neutral character of the Railway, as already secured by International Treaties, none of the officers, servants, or workmen of the Company, whether born in Honduras or elsewhere, shall at any time whilst in the service of the Company be liable to military service, and that no person occupying or being in or upon any of the lands ceded so to the Company, either for the purposes of the Railway or under the Lands Agreement, who is not by birth liable to military service under the laws of Honduras, shall be liable to such service.

The Government reserves the right to repurchase the Railway at the expiration of 50 years, at a price equal to the Company's nominal Share Capital and Debenture Debt, with a bonus addition of 20 per cent.

CONVERSION OF BONDS OF THE EXISTING LOANS.

The Bondholders of the above Loans, upon surrender of their Bonds, will receive in exchange—

For every Bond of £100 of the 1867 or 1870 Loans contracted in London (including unpaid Coupons) and of the Federal Debt, a Share of £100 0 0
For every Bond of £20 of the like Loan, a Share of £20 0 0
For every Bond of £12 in the French Loan of 1869 (with all unpaid Coupons) a Share of . £12 0 0

The Shares issued in exchange for Bonds will bear two per cent. interest during construction on the amount represented by them.

The first Coupon will be payable 1st January, 1875.

THE RAILWAY.

The Line consists of three sections—
1. From Puerto Caballos to La Pimienta, 57 miles.
2. From La Pimienta to Comayagua, 85 miles.
3. From Comayagua to the Bay of Fonseca, 92 miles.

Fifty-seven miles of the Railway, from Puerto Caballos to the Rio Venta, have been made and worked at a profit. One firm alone in 1872, according to the Report of Mr. Brooks, paid for timber-freight the sum of £3,283.

A great deal of costly preliminary work has been done on sections 2 and 3, which will facilitate their rapid construction.

Mr. Brooks, M. Inst. C.E. (for many years Chief Engineer to the Commissioners of the River Tyne), and Mr. Alberga, A.I.E., have carefully inspected the Line already made, and the sections under construction; and certify that the first section is well built and in good order, and that the local traffic is steadily increasing and already worked at a profit.

The Report of Messrs. Brooks and Alberga has been, in all its essential details, fully confirmed by Major-General Gorse, in conjunction with General Wright, who was sent out especially by the Committee of Bondholders, under the authority given them by the meeting of January last.

To provide for the completion and equipment of the Line, the Directors have determined to issue First Mortgage Bonds amounting to Two Millions sterling, bearing interest at 10 per cent.

Messrs. R. G. Huston and Co., of Poplar Plains, Kentucky, U.S., who are an English firm of Railway Contractors of responsibility and eminence (having carried out important contracts on the Ohio and Mississippi, the Cincinnati, Hamilton, and Dayton, and other railways and public works in the United States), have contracted for £9,000 per mile, to construct and complete, within three years from the present time, the unfinished sections of the Railway; one-fourth in cash, and three-fourths in First Mortgage Bonds of the Company, or, at the option of the Company, the whole to be payable in cash. And, in consideration of the assignment to them of all railway plant and material now on the Line, they will guarantee two per cent. interest to the Shareholders during construction.

Considering the revenue to be derived from the freight of mahogany and other woods, from the sale or lease of the adjacent lands and building sites in the vicinity of towns and stations, as well as the profits arising from granting licenses to work, and from working, the mines, there is every reasonable prospect of early and increasing additions to the Company's resources.

For the greater security of the Shareholders a Deed of Trust has been executed, under which the Trustees, pending the completion of the Line, will retain the absolute custody of the Bonds of the existing Loans, and thus preserve intact all the hypothecations appertaining thereto.

The Directors, believing the Bondholders to be fully informed of the various advantages of the undertaking in which their money is embarked, abstain from dilating upon its special features, or the superiority of this over competitive Lines; merely observing, that while this Railway, with a large and profitable way traffic, will only cost £9,000 per mile, the Panama Railway, with its difficult access for shipping, a link between the Atlantic and Pacific Oceans, has cost upwards of £40,000 per mile, and yet, although enjoying no income from way-traffic, after paying £7 per cent. upon a large debenture debt, returned £10½ per cent. in the year 1872 to its shareholders.

The steaming distances from Liverpool to San Francisco, touching at Jamaica, are—by way of Panama, 7,980 miles; Nicaragua, 7,720 miles; Tehuantepec, 7,740 miles; Honduras, 7,320 miles.

The distance between New York and San Francisco, by Panama, is 5,224 miles; by Nicaragua, 4,700 miles; by Tehuantepec, 4,200 miles; by Honduras, 4,121 miles; a saving by way of Honduras as compared with Panama, the only line on which a Railway is already constructed, of 1,103 miles.

The difference in actual distance, coupled with the superiority of ports, the facilities of embarkation and disembarkation, and the connexion with the American coast lines, will effect a saving in time, as compared with the Panama route, of not less than five days between the Atlantic and the Pacific ports of the United States.

Admiral Fitzroy, well known as one of the most eminent among British explorers of the Pacific coast of the American Continent, thus writes in his Report to the Earl of Clarendon, then Prime Minister of England :—" The climate, productions, and population of Honduras are more in favour of a Railway from sea to sea than those of any part of the great Isthmus whatever."

Copies of the conventions between the Honduras Government, Great Britain, France, and the United States, and of all documents and instruments appertaining to the above conversion, including powers from the Provisional President of Honduras to His Excellency Don Carlos Gutierrez and Dr. Bernhard, and the ratifications of the Agreements entered into by them with the Company, together with the Engineer's and Committee's Reports and other documents, and likewise the Memorandum and Articles of Association, may be inspected at the Offices of the Company, where the Prospectuses and Forms of Application for conversion can be obtained.

The treaty between Honduras and Great Britain declares that—

> " In order to secure the construction or permanence of the route or road herein contemplated, and also to secure, for the benefit of mankind, the uninterrupted advantages of such communications from sea to sea, Her Britannic Majesty recognizes the rights of sovereignty and property of Honduras in and over the line of the said road, and for the same reason guarantees positively and efficaciously the entire neutrality of the same. And when the proposed road shall have been completed, Her Britannic Majesty equally engages, in conjunction with the Republic of Honduras, to protect the same from interruption, seizure, or unjust confiscation, from whatsoever quarter the attempt may proceed."

Treaties signed by the Honduras Government with France and the United States contain similar provisions.

The only agreements which have been entered into by or on behalf of the Company are the following, viz. :—

An Agreement dated the 12th day of July, 1873, and made between His Excellency Don Carlos Gutierrez and Dr. Don Charles Ernest Bernhard, for and on behalf of the Government of the said Republic of the one part, and the Company of the other part.

An Agreement of the same date between the same parties.

A Supplemental Agreement dated the 1st of December, 1873,

between the said Dr. Bernhard of the one part, and the Company of the other part.

An Agreement dated the 23rd day of December, 1873, between the Honduras Inter-oceanic Railway Company Limited, of the one part, and Messrs. R. G. Huston and Co., of the other part.

An Agreement dated the 23rd day of December, 1873, between the Company, of the one part, and the Trustees of the Company, of the other part.

An Agreement of the same date, and between the same parties.

No. V.

SHIP RAILWAY ACROSS CENTRAL AMERICA.*

In order that a Ship Railway joining the Atlantic and Pacific Oceans should prove of any real service, it would be necessary that it should be capable of accommodating vessels of at least 1,200 tons burthen, and that it should be so constructed that, if necessary, it could be modified so as to take larger ships.

A vessel carrying 1,200 tons would weigh about 800 tons, and would not exceed 200 feet in length.

We have therefore to provide a Railway capable of carrying a vessel 200 feet long, and weighing, with its cargo, 2,000 tons.

The carriage on which such a ship would be placed should be supported upon a very large number of wheels, to prevent the weight on each being greater than could be dealt with, and for the present we may assume 240 as being about the necessary number.

The number of rails which it would be most economical to adopt would be about six, and that number is taken as the basis of calculation.

The number of wheels on each of the six rails would be forty, and it becomes necessary to consider how these wheels can be taken round curves.

CURVE RADIUS 2000.FT
K ———————————————— K
200 FT

In the case of a curve of 2,000 feet radius, the versed sine of an arc

---

* See page 42.

whose chord is 200 feet, is 2 feet 6 inches; and it therefore follows that the middle wheels, which must be in line with the end wheels on a straight line, must be 2 feet 6 inches out of line in passing round a curve of 2,000 feet radius.

It is quite possible to arrange that the wheels should have a lateral motion equal to this, and also that the axles should be radial or nearly radial to the track; but as the play mentioned is probably as much as could safely be given, it follows that curves of 2,000 feet radius are the sharpest that can be adopted.

The carriage would probably work most easily if the 240 wheels were placed on 60 bogies, those at the ends being fastened to the carriage in the usual manner by bogie pins, and those at other parts of the carriage being fastened by links so as to admit of there being a lateral motion.

Such a carriage could be easily constructed, and would weigh about 600 or 700 tons, and probably cost about £20,000.

Seeing that the total load of carriage, ship, and cargo would be about 2,700 tons, and that the number of wheels is 240, it follows that the load upon each wheel will be between eleven and twelve tons on the average; but as it will be impossible to distribute the load equally among so many wheels, it will be necessary to be prepared for a somewhat greater weight.

The rails of a sufficient strength would therefore weigh not less than 120 lbs. per yard, and the best arrangement would be to lay the six rails each five feet apart, making a total width of twenty-five feet.

The best foundation for this road would probably be wooden cross sleepers thirty feet long, especially at first, and until the banks become quite solid, when, if the timber was found to decay rapidly, it might be replaced with iron; but this need not be done for many years, by which time some definite idea may be formed of the nature and amount of the traffic, and of the points of detail which might be altered with advantage.

The power requisite to pull this carriage and load on a level line would be about 27,000 pounds; and on a gradient of 1 in 200, 57,240; and on a gradient of 1 in 100, 87,480 pounds.

To perform this work with ordinary locomotives would require from four to ten locomotives, according to the state of the rails, whether damp or otherwise.

As the speed need *not* be great, it would appear better to adopt some means by which the locomotives should be independent of the state of the weather. This can be done by laying a rack along the Railway, each locomotive having two toothed wheels which should work in the teeth of the rack; and by working these through gearing, as is done in traction engines and in some contractors' locomotives, it is possible to increase the tractive power of the engine by diminishing the speed.

For the purpose of raising the ship out of the water and placing it on the carriage, a hydraulic lift could be made use of, similar to those used for floating graving docks. By this system a ship is raised bodily out of water and floated away on a pontoon for repairs; and for the purposes of this Railway, a ship could likewise be lifted and placed on a carriage for transport. The details of the process would be varied, but the principle would be precisely the same, and seems superior for this purpose to any description of inclined road like a patent slip.

If these methods be adopted, there can be no difficulty in constructing or working a Ship Railway, provided the means at the engineer's disposal be unlimited; and it only remains to estimate the cost of such a line, and to consider whether the traffic would be likely to give a proper return on the capital.

To estimate the cost of earthwork and bridges without a section, is impossible, and a section of an ordinary railway with curves of 330 feet radius gives very little idea of what the section would be if curves of 2000 feet radius were used. The estimate of this part of the scheme must therefore be taken as a good guess, probably not very far wrong, but possibly somewhat wide of the truth.

In constructing such a line, high banks should not be used, as they are liable to settlement, and it will therefore be necessary to allow a larger proportion than usual for cuttings.

Tunnels are, of course, out of the question, and this again will occasion an additional amount of cutting and increased expense.

Under all circumstances it would not be safe to estimate less than 400,000 cubic yards of cutting per mile.

The cost of one mile of permanent way, constructed according to the sketches on the following page, would be:

Rails	.	.	tons	566 at	£12	£6792
Fishes	.	.	,,	44 ,,	14	616
Fastenings	.	.	,,	35 ,,	20	700
Rack, average	.	.	,,	300 ,,	24	7200
Sleepers	.	.	Nos.	1760 ,,	90s.	7920
Ballast	.	.	Cy.	53,000 ,,	3s.	7950
Rail-laying	.	.	Ly.	1760 ,,	10s.	880
						£32,058

Cross Section of Cutting.

Cross Section of Permanent Way.

Plan of Permanent Way.

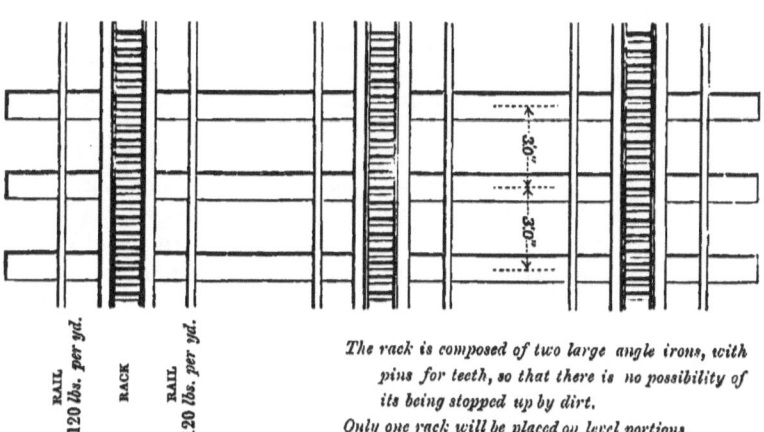

The rack is composed of two large angle irons, with pins for teeth, so that there is no possibility of its being stopped up by dirt.
Only one rack will be placed on level portions.

The allowance for Bridges may be taken at per mile £10,000

The cost of one mile of Earthwork would be, cubic yards 400,000, at 2/6 . . £50,000

These figures, which may be taken as something near the mark, give the means of calculating the cost of a line 230 miles in length, which would be the length of a line across Honduras.

The Estimate would be as follows:

230 miles	Earthwork.	at	£50,000	=	£11,500,000
230 ,,	Bridges .	,,	10,000	=	2,300,000
5 ,,	Passing Places .	,,	50,000	=	250,000
235 ,,	Permanent Way	,,	32,000	=	7,520,000
100 Carriages		,,	20,000	=	2,000,000
400 Locomotives		,,	3,500	=	1,400,000
Docks and Hydraulic Lifts .				.	430,000
Workshops, &c.				.	400,000
					£25,800,000

To this must be added the cost of engineering, management, interest on capital during construction, &c., making a total capital of say £30,000,000, which cannot be considered, after all, an extraordinary amount, when the enormous advantages which will accrue to the commercial world from the opening of a Ship Railway across Central America areborne in mind.

According to Official Reports presented to both Houses of Parliament by Her Majesty's Government, the total tonnage cleared for shipment round Cape Horn is as follows:

To and from	Great Britain . .	. 16	millions of tons
,,	other European Countries	10	,,
,,	Central America .	. 8	,,
,,	United States of America	20	,,
		54	millions of tons.

Now, supposing that less than one-half of the said tonnage, viz. twenty-five millions, passes over the intended Ship Railway across Honduras, and a sum of four dollars or sixteen shillings only is charged per ton, leaving, after deducting fifty cent. for working expenses, two dollars or eight shillings net per ton, the Ship Railway would pay a net sum of ten millions sterling per annum, which would be more than three times the amount required to pay ten per cent. interest upon the outlay of thirty millions sterling.

It is therefore evident that a Ship Railway across Honduras would be a profitable enterprise for the Government as well as a great boon for the commercial interest of the world.

JAMES BRUNLEES.

5, Victoria Street, Westminster,
    8th May, 1871.

SHIP RAILWAY ACROSS CENTRAL AMERICA.

To His Excellency DON CARLOS GUTIERREZ,
    Honduras Minister in London.

EXCELLENCY,—

In order that a Ship Railway joining the Atlantic and Pacific Oceans should prove of service, it is necessary that it should be capable of accommodating vessels of 1200 tons burthen, and so constructed that, if necessary, it could be modified so as to take larger ships.

A vessel carrying 1200 tons would weigh about 800 tons, and would not exceed 200 feet in length.

The Railway, therefore, will have to be capable of carrying a vessel 200 feet long, and weighing with its cargo 2000 tons.

The carriage to be constructed on which the ship will be placed must be supported upon a very large number of wheels, to prevent the weight on each being greater than could be dealt with, and 240 is therefore found to be the requisite number.

The number of rails which it would be most economical to adopt would be six.

The number of wheels on each of the six rails will be forty, and it becomes necessary to explain how these wheels can be taken round curves.

In the case of a curve of 2000 feet radius, the versed sine of an arc whose chord is 200 feet, is 2 feet 6 inches; and it therefore follows that the middle wheels would be 2 feet 6 inches out of line in passing round a curve of that radius.

The wheels will be so arranged as to have a lateral motion equal to this, and the axles will be radial or nearly radial to the track; but as the play mentioned is as much as could be given, it follows that curves of 2000 feet radius are the sharpest that can be adopted.

The carriage will work most easily by the 240 wheels being on sixty bogies, those at the ends being fastened to the carriage in the usual manner by bogie pins, and those at other parts of the carriage being fastened by links, so as to admit of there being a lateral motion.

Such a carriage can be constructed, and will weigh about 600 or 700 tons, and cost about £20,000.

Seeing that the total load of carriage, ship, and cargo, would be about 2700 tons, and the number of wheels is 240, it follows that the load upon each wheel will average between eleven and twelve tons; but as it is impossible to distribute the load equally over so many wheels, it is necessary to be prepared for a somewhat greater weight.

The rails of a sufficient strength would therefore weigh not less than 120 lbs. per yard, and the six rails will be laid each 5 feet apart, making a total width of twenty-five feet.

The best foundation for this road will be wooden cross sleepers thirty feet long, especially at first and until the banks become quite solid, and the timber when decayed might be replaced with iron, but this need not be done for many years.

The power requisite to pull this carriage and load on a level line will be about 27,000 pounds, and on a gradient of 1 in 200, 57,240, and on a gradient of 1 in 100, 87,480 pounds.

To perform this work would require from four to ten locomotives, according to the state of the rails, whether damp or otherwise.

As the speed will *not* require to be great, means will be adopted by which the locomotives should be almost independent of the state of the weather. This will be done by laying a rack along the railway, each locomotive having two toothed wheels which should work in the teeth of the rack; and by working these through gearing, as is done in traction engines, the tractive power of the engine will be increased by diminishing the speed.

For the purpose of raising the ship out of the water and placing it on the carriage, Clark's hydraulic lift will be made use of, similar to those used for floating graving docks. By this system a ship is raised bodily out of water and floated away on a pontoon for repairs; and for the purposes of this Railway, a ship will likewise be lifted and placed on a carriage for transport. The details of the process would be varied, but the principle would be precisely the same, and seems superior for this purpose to any description of inclined road like a patent slip.

By the adoption of these methods, there can be no difficulty in constructing and working the Ship Railway, and it is only necessary to consider whether the traffic would be likely to give a proper return on the capital.

In constructing such a line high banks cannot be used, as they

...ble to settlement, and it will therefore be necessary to make ...r proportion than usual of cuttings.

...ding to Official Reports presented to both Houses of Parliament... Her Majesty's Government and other statistics, the total ...cleared annually for shipment round Cape Horn is as...

...m Great Britain	16 millions of tons.	
„ other European Countries	10	„ „
„ Central America	8	„ „
„ United States of America	20	„ „
Total	54 millions of tons.	

Now, estimating that less than one-half of the said tonnage, viz., twenty-five millions, passes over the intended Ship Railway across Honduras, and a sum of four dollars or sixteen shillings only is charged per ton, leaving, after deducting fifty per cent. for working expenses, two dollars or eight shillings net per ton, the Ship Railway would pay a net sum of ten millions sterling per annum.

It is therefore evident that a Ship Railway across Honduras would be a profitable enterprise for the Government as well as a great boon for the commercial interest of the world.

JAMES BRUNLEES.

..., Victoria Street, Westminster; 21st March, 1872.

To His Excellency DON CARLOS GUTIERREZ,
    Honduras Minister in London.

EXCELLENCY,—

    I concur with Mr. Brunlees in the opinion that, under the conditions assigned by him in reference to curves, gradients, and security of road-bed from settlement, a Ship Railway can be constructed and efficiently worked across the Isthmus in Honduras, so as to connect the Oceans East and West.

    I see no difficulty in carrying out adequate mechanical arrangements, such as are described in outline by Mr. Brunlees—whether for lifting ships out of the water by hydraulic lifts, for placing them into trucks for transport, for conveying them along the line of Railway, and for afterwards lowering them again into the water.

    The precise constructive details can, I suppose, only be settled definitely after the survey of the line and of the ports has been completed.

(Signed)   EDWARD WOODS.

Storey's Gate, Westminster; April 3rd, 1872.

Cross Section of Cutting.

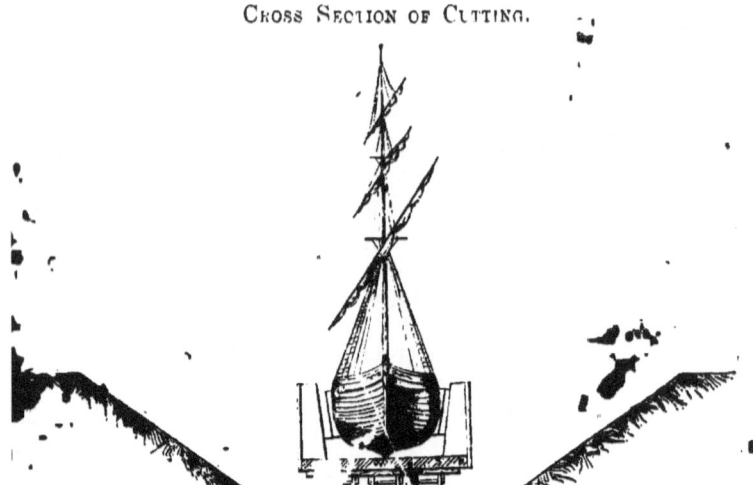

Cross Section of Permanent Way.

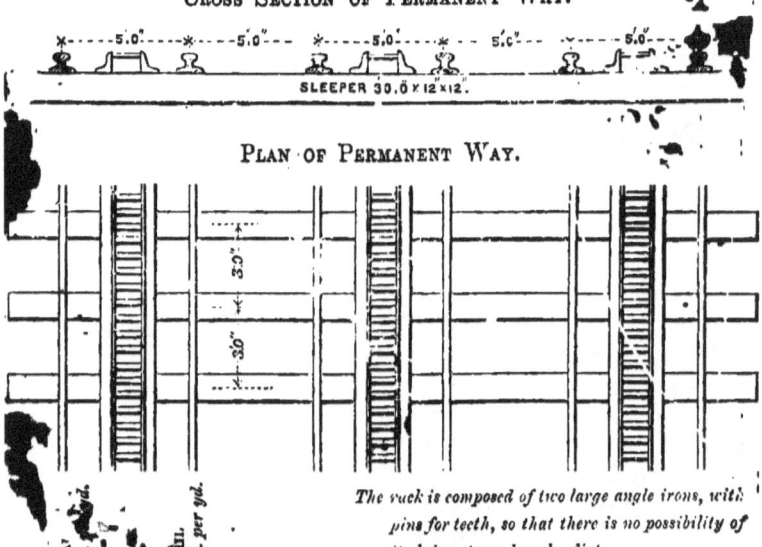

The rack is composed of two large angle irons, with pins for teeth, so that there is no possibility of its being stopped up by dirt.
Only one rack will be placed on level portions.

www.ingramcontent.com/pod-product-compliance
Lightning Source LLC
Chambersburg PA
CBHW030434190426
43202CB00036B/845